at the
kitchen table

at the
kitchen table

simple low-waste recipes for family & friends

Megan Davies

photography by Clare Winfield

RYLAND PETERS & SMALL
LONDON • NEW YORK

DEDICATION

To the bravest and strongest woman I know, Katy Gurney.

Senior designer Megan Smith
Senior editor Miriam Catley
Head of production Patricia Harrington
Art director Leslie Harrington
Editorial director Julia Charles
Publisher Cindy Richards

Food stylist Megan Davies
Props stylist Polly Webb-Wilson
Food styling assistants Jojo Jackson and Elle McCann
Illustrations Megan Davies

Published in 2020 by
Ryland Peters & Small
20–21 Jockey's Fields, London
WC1R 4BW and
341 E 116th St, New York
NY 10029
www.rylandpeters.com

10 9 8 7 6 5 4 3 2 1

US ISBN: 978-1-78879-199-1
UK ISBN: 978-1-78879-233-2

Printed and bound in China

US Library of Congress CIP data has been applied for.

NOTES

- Both British (Metric) and American (Imperial plus US cups) measurements are included here for your convenience, however it is important to work with one set of measurements and not alternate between themwithin a recipe.
- All spoon measurements are level unless otherwise specified.
- All eggs are medium (UK) or large (US), unless specified as large, in which case US extra-large should be used. Uncooked or partially cooked eggs should not be served to the very old, frail, young children, pregnant women or those with compromised immune systems.
- Ovens should be preheated to the specified temperatures. We recommend using an oven thermometer.
- Whenever butter is used, use unsalted unless otherwise stated.

contents

INTRODUCTION

This book began its life as a small supper club, held in my friends' bakery, Pophams, in London. The idea was to move away from perfectly-portioned plates, multiple courses and fine-dining. I wanted to go 'back to the kitchen table' and to cook food that was both nostalgic and innovative; to make simple meals, offered in big bowls, and to encourage diners to sit at one large table and serve their neighbour before themselves. It was also important to me that there was a low-waste focus in the kitchen, where possible. We served Potato Peel Crisps (see page 121) with saucisson on small chopping boards so guests could help themselves as they arrived. Next, was a big feasting main course of Braised Short Rib (see page 94), Roasted Carrots & Legumes (see page 123), mash (having used the peel for the crisps mentioned earlier) and a big Red Cos & Seed Salad with Polenta Croutons (see pages 110–1). Roasted Mixed Squash with Almonds & Tarragon (see page 78) was served alongside. I made an Orange, Hazelnut & Caraway Pavlova (see page 138) for dessert and Spiced Mint Tea (see page 45) to finish things off.

My husband, Hal, helped every night, and my sister, Summer, was on washing up once or twice, too. It was a family affair; literally so in the kitchen and it certainly felt like it at the table. People seemed to enjoy it, and, for me, it just felt right to serve food that way, it was like being at home.

I come from a big, loud, hungry family where the tables have chairs from upstairs squeezed in, there are squished-up elbows resting on edges, clinking glasses, noses lifting to get a whiff of the imminent meal (all sounding like idyllic, nuclear bliss I know, but don't be fooled) and then generous piles of grub served up, passed around and shared. My grandparents, parents, aunts and uncles are all genuinely brilliant home cooks.

Whilst some are more effortlessly skilled than others, they all 'properly' enjoy food and cooking in all its forms, taking delight in even the simplest piece of toast, through to a show-stopping dish or feast. They are who I learnt from as a child, they gave me the confidence to cook intuitively, make fridge-foraged meals, be inventive with leftovers and not be scared to 'swap in' ingredients and just use what you've got. 'It'll be great!' they say, and it usually is.

I've written this book based on my childhood experiences with food and my love of cooking, paired with a somewhat unsettled conscience regarding food waste and my carbon footprint.

We have a huge (and quite frankly terrifying) responsibility to radically change the way that we run this planet, but with all the will in the world, it's hard to do so when you have a job, bills to pay, possibly a car, children, enjoy buying new clothes or flying. When we fully realize how much energy we use and waste we create it's easy to wonder how we'll be able to do anything at all to help. This book aims to take small steps in the right direction, to do little, achievable things first, whilst we tackle the dilemmas of making the bigger personal changes. Not wasting food, or at least wasting less food should be easy.

I've tried to adopt the way my grandparents and their parents managed their kitchens and food. They made satisfying, nourishing meals; they cherished meat, fats and fresh produce when it was on the menu and made use of every part of not only the animal but also all other ingredients.

Stretch your food, with the help of the 'swap ins' and 'leftovers' notes on each recipe. These tips will encourage you to use what you've got at home before you go out and buy more and to make inventive new meals with scraps and scrapings

as opposed to just piling them on toast (although I do love most leftovers on toast, it has to be said).

Some of the creations are based on leftovers from another recipe, for example, Chilli & Chocolate Con Carne (see page 101) doubles up with Chilli & Lentil Parcels (see page 67), where part of the parcel filling is leftover chilli from the original recipe.

Use the 'mini recipes' section (see pages 9–13) for some simple tips on stretching things that might otherwise be thrown away. They're by no means revolutionary or original ideas, just a little list of nifty examples that might help.

The chapters have been broken up into fluid sections that work for varying lifestyles and eating habits (if you want fish and chips or pasta for breakfast, though, be my guest; just make sure you save any leftovers for lunch!). I've also set out some menu plans (see pages 154–7) with combinations of dishes that I cook at home, often at the weekends or for dinner parties, should you like some inspiration – that, or make your own, there are tons of options! Enjoy the recipes, cook and share them with loved ones, and last, but not least, get excited about what remains on the plate in the fridge for tomorrow!

My cooking notes
- Invest in a good non-stick baking sheet and frying pan/skillet – you'll use less baking paper or foil in the long run, and that's a good thing.
- Use an upside-down plate instead of clingfilm/plastic wrap in the fridge. Alternatively, invest in some long-life covers and containers.
- Cook and eat seasonal (and local) ingredients when possible and where affordable. They'll taste better, be cheaper (most of the time) and will have hopefully not travelled so far.

- Make sure you check for any prep instructions alongside the ingredients before cooking.
- When soft herbs are chopped, do so with leaves and stalks, unless stalks are particularly hardy.
- Use extra virgin olive oil for salad dressings and finishing touches, not cooking. Use olive oil for cooking, frying (not high temperature), marinading and coating for oven cooking, and then vegetable (preferably rapeseed) oil for high-heat frying, and roasting/oven cooking too.
- Most vegetable oils in the UK are rapeseed oil so no need to buy the more expensive, rapeseed oil, just check the back of the veg oil bottles.
- Store eggs, tomatoes and fruit at room temperature (unless it's very hot).
- Taste, season, now taste and season again.

MINI RECIPES

These little recipe ideas are designed to help you to make use of the likes of lurking lemon halves, leftover condiments and souring milk. These are brief guides, so get experimenting to see what you can stretch and make use of.

squeezed citrus

When you've just squeezed citrus halves for the juice in a recipe and see no use for them, don't throw them away! There is still lots of flavour in the fruit. To make use of the squeezed fruit, cut it up into slices, wedges, chunks (whatever), and add to a jug/pitcher. Fill with water, add any fresh herbs you might have floating around and store in the fridge for up to 2 days, topping up with water as you get through it. The fruit (and herbs) will start to turn after 48 hours (give or take), so just compost them at the point they taste a little past it. Or, chop them up into chunks and freeze in a reusable bag, then add to that bag as and when you end up with more squeezed citrus fruits. The frozen fruit can later be added to glasses, re-usable bottles for on-the-go, mugs of hot water, herbal teas, cordials or spirit/mixer drinks.

dried citrus

We have Mark Curtis to thank for this great tip, having served me one of the loveliest gin and tonics I've had in a while. Cut wrinkling oranges, limes, lemons and grapefruit into thin slices (a serrated fruit knife is best, I find) and place them on a baking sheet in a single layer. Bake for several hours (overnight or all day is preferable) at about 60°C/140°F until they are fully dried out, and slightly darkened. Store in an airtight container and pop a couple into any spirit and mixer with ice. They infuse the drink with a richer, more earthy flavour than fresh citrus, that develops as you get down the glass, glorious. I've been making these for years, but for my Christmas tree. Seems a bit lame in comparison...

kind of pickled greens

Use up aging cucumbers, courgettes/zucchini or other greens by cutting away any really soggy sections, and then slicing thinly. Cover with white wine or rice wine vinegar, a pinch of dried chilli/hot red pepper flakes and a little seasoning. Serve on toast or alongside dishes such as Sweet Potato Baked Eggs (see page 29), Chilli & Chocolate Con Carne (see page 101), Asian Chicken Salad (see page 92), Saucy Coconut Noodles with Prawns (see page 63) or the Roasted Onion, Mixed Tomato & Chickpea Curry (see page 77).

pickling veg

Whenever you prep veg and are about to throw the ends away, don't! Give them a rinse and then pop them in a sterilized jar (with a lid, also sterilized and ready to seal) and some pickling liquor. Do so with the odds and ends of carrots, radishes, beetroots, fennel, garlic and onions.

100 g/½ cup caster/granulated sugar
250 ml/1 cup plus 1 tablespoon vinegar (any kind)
whole spices, such as cloves, star anise, coriander seeds, fennel seeds or peppercorns (optional)

Put the sugar, vinegar and 100 ml/⅓ cup plus 1 tablespoon water, together with a few spices if you have them, into a small saucepan and bring to the boil over a medium heat, so the sugar dissolves before the liquid boils. Let the liquid simmer for a minute, then remove from the heat and let cool. Pour over the veg in a sterilized glass jar, seal and store in a cool, dry place. If unopened, it should last for up to 2 months. Once opened, I'd say 2–3 weeks.

pastry scraps & chutney bites

It's really tempting to throw away pastry when you only have a small quantity of it left, but it freezes well so don't throw it out. Alternatively, tear it up into pieces, pile a teaspoon of chutney in the centre, top with some grated or crumbled cheese (any kind) and bake for 20–30 minutes until golden and bubbling. This works with puff or shortcrust, and don't be afraid to try out different combinations. Caramelized onions are great too, as is pesto. You can also do so with sweet toppings, such as jams/jellies and fresh fruits, with an extra sprinkling of sugar on top before baking. Serve them as snacks, canapés, desserts or just a treat for being so industrious!

leftover cornichon jars

I always have cornichons at home, and am therefore constantly left with jars of the vinegar they live in. Use up this flavoursome liquor either in salad dressings, or by re-filling the jar with some fresh chilli/chile, garlic and shallot slices and send them back to the fridge, so they do a mini pickle until you need them for cooking, adding to sandwiches, Ploughman's boards and the like. They won't last as long as properly pickled veg, but they're not bad!

used tea bags & coffee

Make iced tea or coffee! This is obviously more likely an appealing option in the warmer months, but give it a go and see what you think.

Add a couple of used black tea bags to a jug/pitcher of water with some lemon (use the pieces in your freezer, if you have any) and a dash of honey, if you want some sweetness. Stir to combine and store in the fridge. It's a great refreshing drink, and you can also treat it like Pimm's – if you're serving it at the table for a lunch, for example, top it up with fresh mint, strawberries, apple and more lemon.

Alternatively, add a few tea leaves to homemade jam/jelly. I sometimes add them to my Balsamic Strawberries that go with the Rice Pudding (see page 135) and it's quite lovely. Earl Grey works particularly well.

Iced coffee is a great refreshment, and even better made at home without the ridiculous price tag from a coffee shop. Save the leftover coffee from a cafetiere in the fridge and when you're ready, pour about the amount you would of vodka or gin in a drink (a finger or two) into a glass over plenty of ice and top up with milk of your choice. That, or water if you don't want a latte-style drink.

bits & bones for stock

If you have a chicken carcass, meat or fish bones that post-meal you don't want to throw away, but don't have the time to deal with, simply freeze to make stock another time. Place the bones in a freezer bag for up to 1 month and then defrost when you have a few hours at home. You'll need the following to throw in a large saucepan with the bones and water: onion, celery, carrot, garlic cloves, black peppercorns, bay leaves, thyme and parsley. Bring the water to the boil and let simmer for a few hours (skimming and discarding any scum that floats on the surface).

crisps or cornflakes

Crisps and cornflakes are an excellent way to add texture to toppings. For savoury dishes, scrunch up crisps and fold them through breadcrumbs or grated cheese to spread on top of pasta bakes, moussakas or lasagnes, corrupted versions, I know, but tasty. For sweet toppings, use cornflakes in the same way as the crisps, on crumbles and cobblers, in flapjacks and so on.

'bird food' crackers

You can make crackers using mixed seeds (or even one or two types if you have a glut of them), oats and a little liquid.

50 g/½ cup oats
100 g/3½ oz. mixed seeds
2 tablespoons runny honey or maple syrup
1 tablespoon oil
pinch each of salt and freshly ground black pepper

Preheat the oven to 170°C fan/190°C/375°F/Gas 5. Mix the oats with 50 ml/3½ tablespoons water in a bowl until the oats soak up the water, then add the seeds, honey or maple syrup and oil with a pinch of seasoning. Mix well to combine and spread onto a lined baking sheet. Press down using the back of a spoon to compress and bake in the preheated oven for 40 minutes–1 hour. Allow to cool completely, then break up and enjoy! Try these out adding ½ teaspoon of different nut oils, different ground spices for flavouring and so on. They can be sweet or savoury so play around. I also love them broken up and sprinkled on things, like a crunchy garnish. Try with Indian Scrambled Eggs (see page 36), Baked Rosemary & Nutmeg Nectarines (see page 132) or Rice Pudding (see page 135).

stale pastries & bread

Use old pastries like you would stale bread – rip them up into croutons and bake. That's not anything new, but use them in roasting recipes, such as The Best Roast Chicken (see page 88), where the croissant croutons soak up the chicken juices underneath, and go brown and crisp on top.

souring milk

Souring milk is one of the most annoying things to find in the fridge. Whilst it's not great in a cup of tea, you can still use it in baking. As long as there isn't any mould, it will be okay to cook with. One of the simplest ways souring milk can be used in a recipe is in place of buttermilk. Try using it in the Soda Bread Boulders (see page 32) or the dumplings in the Veggie Stew (see page 82) and see how you go.

You can also use it to marinade meat, I like it with chicken best – again, as you would use buttermilk or yogurt with a load of spices to marinade chicken, do it with soured milk!

dusk or dawn

For mornings, brunches or refreshments,
a second breakfast or those evenings when
you just feel like something lighter.

roasted buckwheat & yogurt

I had to make a dessert for a load of guests a few years back, with nothing much at home. I had half a pack of buckwheat, which I threw in a pan with some oil and added spices and sugar. Once it was toasted, it made a crunchy, crumbly brittle that I served with baked stone fruits and yogurt. It was a success but digests better when par-boiled, hence this development. You can prep the roasted buckwheat ahead and store it as you would granola. Buckwheat is also gluten-free so this is a great, crunchy and wholesome breakfast or dessert topping for coeliacs and gluten-free eaters too.

100 g/½ cup buckwheat
1½ teaspoons olive oil
2 teaspoons runny honey,
   plus extra to serve
a pinch of sea salt
strained Greek yogurt, to serve
fresh fruit, to serve

SERVES 4
TIME 20 minutes

Preheat the oven to 180°C fan/200°C/400°F/Gas 6.

Bring a saucepan of water to the boil. Add the buckwheat and cook on a rapid boil for 5 minutes. Drain and rinse under cold water and then spread out onto a non-stick baking sheet.

Transfer to the top shelf of the preheated oven and bake for 5 minutes. Remove from the oven, add the oil and honey to the buckwheat with a pinch of sea salt and gently mix. They ping around a bit so watch out.

Return the coated buckwheat to the oven and roast for a further 10 minutes, folding halfway through. Once ready, transfer to a plate and let cool, mixing occasionally to avoid it sticking (although some clumps are nice). Serve on top of yogurt and fresh fruit, and top with an extra drizzle of honey.

Swap ins
You can use any yogurt you like, and any fruit you like – I love it with apple, pear, blueberries, strawberries or nectarines, depending on the time of year.

Leftovers
Store the fully cooled, roasted buckwheat in an airtight container at room temperature, for up to 3 days.

3 FRITTATAS

Frittatas have to be the best fridge-raid meals around. You can chuck almost anything into them and they'll do you proud. Please use the additions to the egg in these recipes as a guide and add in whatever you have to hand.

six herb frittata

6 eggs
2 tablespoons milk or water
30 g/1 oz. fresh herbs, such as parsley, basil, dill, tarragon, mint or coriander/cilantro
sea salt and freshly ground black pepper
olive oil, for cooking

SERVES 2–4
TIME 15 minutes

Preheat the grill/broiler to high.

Whisk the eggs and milk with a fork and season.

Roughly tear up the herbs and stalks with your hands, discarding any tough stalks. Add the herbs to the eggs and whisk once more to combine.

Add a drizzle of oil to a small, non-stick frying pan/skillet and put over a low-medium heat. When hot, add the egg and herb mixture to the pan. Let the frittata start to cook and set for 8 minutes untouched. Using a heat-resistant silicone spatula, run around the edge of the frittata to check the underside colour. If it's coloured too quickly, reduce the heat slightly, and if it's not set at all, increase.

Once the frittata is almost set but there is uncooked egg in the centre, transfer the pan from the hob to the grill/broiler and cook for 1–2 minutes, until just set. Remove the pan from the grill/broiler and let sit for a couple of minutes. Transfer to a board and serve.

roast dinner frittata

6 eggs
2 tablespoons milk or water
150–200 g/5½–7 oz. roast lunch leftovers (vegetables, and meat, if you have it)
10 g/⅓ oz. freshly chopped parsley
10 g/⅓ oz. Parmesan
sea salt and freshly ground black pepper
olive oil, for cooking

SERVES 2–4
TIME 15 minutes

Preheat the grill/broiler to high.

Whisk the eggs and milk with a fork and season. Roughly slice the roast lunch leftovers.

Add a drizzle of oil to a medium, non-stick frying pan/skillet and put over a high heat. Add the roast lunch leftovers. Fry for 1–2 minutes until piping hot. Meanwhile, add the chopped parsley to the egg mixture and mix to combine.

Reduce the heat to low-medium and add the seasoned egg mixture to the pan. Briefly space out the leftovers within the egg mix and then leave to set for about 8 minutes.

Once the frittata is almost set, but there is uncooked egg in the centre, grate the Parmesan on top, then transfer to the grill/broiler and cook for a further 2–3 minutes, until golden on top and set. Remove from the grill/broiler and set aside for a couple of minutes before transferring to a board and serve.

potato, peas, spring onions & feta

300 g/10½ oz. Charlotte or new
    potatoes
6 eggs
2 tablespoons milk or water
3 spring onions/scallions, thinly sliced
80 g/⅔ cup frozen peas
100 g/¾ cup feta cheese
sea salt and freshly ground black
    pepper
olive oil, for cooking

SERVES 2–4
TIME 35 minutes

Preheat the grill/broiler to high.

Quarter the potatoes lengthways into 2–3-cm/
¾–1¼-inch wedges, then add to a small saucepan
of salted water and bring to the boil. Once boiling,
cook for 5 minutes on a rapid boil. Drain and rinse
under cold water.

Whisk the eggs and milk with a fork and season.
Add the spring onions/scallions along with the
frozen peas, and crumble in the feta.

Once the potatoes are drained, let them steam
for a minute in the colander, and heat a drizzle
of oil in a medium, non-stick frying pan/skillet on
a medium-high heat. Once hot, add the potatoes
and fry for 5–8 minutes, tossing occasionally, until
they're golden brown and tender.

Reduce the heat to low-medium and add
the egg mixture to the pan. Briefly space out
the potatoes and then leave to set for 8 minutes.

Once the frittata is almost set, but there is
uncooked egg in the centre, transfer to the grill/
broiler and cook for 2–3 minutes, until golden on
top and set. Remove from the grill/broiler and set
aside for a couple of minutes before transferring
to a board and serve.

Swap ins
You can add so many fresh or leftover
ingredients to a frittata, so no rules here
– you can't go too far wrong.

Leftovers
Let it cool completely, then store in an
airtight container in the fridge for up to
2 days and eat cold. Great for picnics, desk
lunches or just a no-cook supper.

bay-roasted grapes with black pepper ricotta on toast

5–6 fresh bay leaves
300 g/10½ oz. red grapes
4 slices sourdough or rye bread
250 g/1 cup ricotta
½ teaspoon cracked black pepper
sea salt
olive oil, for drizzling

SERVES 2–4
TIME 20 minutes

I came up with this dish when I was private cheffing in Portugal a few years ago. There were some tired-looking grapes in the fruit bowl and no clients to cook for that lunchtime, so I chucked them in the oven with some bay leaves and the rest is history. To me, the combination is perfect; those blistering skins and warm juices trickling down over creamy ricotta.

Preheat the oven to 210°C fan/230°C/450°F/Gas 8.

Scatter the bay leaves onto a small baking sheet and top with the grapes. Drizzle with some olive oil and a sprinkling of sea salt. Place on the middle shelf of the preheated oven and bake for 15 minutes until the grapes are soft, coloured and the skins are bursting.

Meanwhile, toast the slices of bread, then mix the ricotta with the black pepper and a pinch of salt and pile on top of the toast. Once the grapes are ready, pile on top of the ricotta toast and make sure you pour any pan juices over too.

Swap ins
Dried bay leaves are fine, then any other colour of grape, pitted cherries or quartered plums instead of red grapes work well. Swap ricotta for cream cheese or a mild, soft goat's cheese.

Leftovers
Save your roasted bay leaves (for up to 4 days in an airtight container in the fridge) and chuck them in your next stew, roasting pan or ragu.

proper 'baked' beans on toast

You can't beat Heinz baked beans, and this isn't trying to replicate it; here, I'm sharing a fresher, slightly lighter version to serve on toast, possibly with some halloumi, or even just some pesto on the side. I love it for a late breakfast or early supper, whatever the weather. Make it the night before a brunch and reheat on the hob too.

2 brown onions, finely sliced
1 red chilli/chile
3 garlic cloves, grated
½ teaspoon smoked paprika
1 teaspoon light brown muscovado
    sugar
2 tablespoons red wine vinegar
2 tablespoons Worcestershire sauce
600 g/21 oz. fresh tomatoes,
    roughly chopped
10 g/⅓ oz. fresh parsley
2 x 400-g/14-oz. cans butter/lima
    beans, drained and rinsed
1 x 400-g/14-oz. can haricot beans,
    drained and rinsed
6 slices bread of your choice
sea salt and freshly ground
    black pepper
oil, for cooking
salad, to serve
fried halloumi, to serve

SERVES 6
TIME 45 minutes

Add a glug of oil to a large saucepan over a medium heat and, once hot, add the onion. Allow them to sizzle gently for 10 minutes, until softened.

Pierce the chilli/chile a few times, but otherwise leave it whole. Set aside.

Once the onions have softened, add the garlic, paprika and sugar and cook for 1 minute. Next, add the vinegar and Worcestershire sauce and bubble for 30 seconds, then pile in the tomatoes and chilli/chile.

Mix well to combine, simmer for 5 minutes, then add all the drained beans. Simmer gently for a further 20 minutes.

Roughly chop the parsley (stalks and all), then toast the bread.

Season the beans, then taste and add more seasoning if needed. Fold through the parsley and serve the beans on toast.

Swap ins
Use a 400-g/14-oz. can of chopped tomatoes instead of fresh, and garlic paste is fine too. A small pinch of dried chilli/hot red pepper flakes can replace the fresh, and any sugar is fine but preferably brown. The red wine vinegar can be replaced with any other vinegar, and coriander/cilantro is lovely in place of (or in addition to) the parsley.

Leftovers
Reheat (until piping hot) and serve on fresh toast again, or add a can of chopped tomatoes, heat up and use as a shakshuka base or pasta sauce.

breakfast
for an army

8 chipolatas
4 rashers/slices bacon
4 slices black pudding
10 g/⅓ oz. freshly chopped parsley
1 garlic clove, grated
20 g/1½ tablespoons butter,
    at room temperature
4 Portobello mushrooms
250 g/9 oz. cherry tomatoes
    on the vine
4 slices sourdough
4 eggs
sea salt and freshly ground
    black pepper
olive oil, for drizzling

2 large non-stick baking sheets

SERVES 4
TIME 45 minutes

Swap ins

Use vine tomatoes instead of cherry tomatoes, just cut them in half. Instead of the Portobello, white or chestnut mushrooms work well; just microwave the parsley butter and then pour over the mushrooms once on the sheet. The bread by no means has to be sourdough either, just whatever you like or have at home.

Leftovers

You can chop up the cooked bacon, sausages, mushrooms and tomatoes and turn them into a fry-up frittata (use the frittata recipes on page 18 for guidance) or add to a pizza for extra toppings!

An army of four is still an army when it comes to making a fry-up. This recipe focuses on the ease of throwing almost everything onto two baking sheets, so you don't have lots to wash up – if you have more than four people, divide the recipe ingredients by four, and then multiply by the number of people eating, so there is the right amount of food for everyone expecting a good old full(ish) English.

Preheat the oven to 200°c fan/220°C/425°F/Gas 7.

Add the chipolatas, bacon and black pudding to one of the large, non-stick baking sheets, then drizzle with oil and season with black pepper. Place on the top shelf of the preheated oven for 25 minutes.

Add the parsley, garlic and butter to a bowl and mash to combine. Divide the butter mixture into four and spread onto the mushrooms (gill-side facing up). Put the mushrooms onto the second large baking sheet, along with the tomatoes (keep on the vine).

Once the meaty baking sheet has had its time, remove from the oven and transfer the cooked chipolatas, bacon and black pudding onto the second sheet with the veggies and then place the bread slices onto the hot and oily sheet (that you've just emptied).

Put the second, and now full, baking sheet into the oven for a further 15 minutes, on the middle shelf.

Note: If the bacon is fully cooked and crispy already at this point, transfer it to a plate and set aside.

Swipe the slices of bread around the original/meaty sheet to soak up the oil and juices. Space out the slices on the tray, and then using your fingers (or a knife), pull out the centre of each piece of bread. Add the centres to the sheet too, like large croutons, and when 10 minutes cooking time for sheet two remains, crack an egg into each hole you've created in the slices. Add a pinch of seasoning to the whole sheet. Carefully place the egg sheet onto the top shelf of the oven and bake for 6–8 minutes, until the bread is light golden and the eggs are cooked. Serve immediately.

sweet potato baked eggs

4 sweet potatoes
1 teaspoon dried chilli/hot red
    pepper flakes, plus extra to serve
4 eggs
40 g/1½ oz. pumpkin seeds
20 g/¾ oz. freshly chopped
    coriander/cilantro
sea salt and freshly ground
    black pepper
vegetable oil, for cooking

SERVES 4
TIME 1 hour 10 minutes

Swap ins

Large Maris Piper potatoes, or even a butternut squash half, with the seeds scooped out. Crack the egg into the hole! Crispy chillies/hot red pepper flakes in oil (from large supermarkets and Asian supermarkets) are great here too as a replacement or addition to the dried chilli/hot red pepper flakes.

Leftovers

Once cool, chop up the leftovers, mix with some chopped fresh herbs and shape into burger-style patties. Chill for 20 minutes to firm up, then fry into little sweet potato cakes.

Most things, in my opinion, either are or should be a vessel for the glorious egg. This recipe is a more filling version of traditional baked eggs in ramekins. I've always loved sweet potato and chilli/chile together, and eggs and chilli/chile together too, so why not add them all and make a meal out of it?! This is a great one to throw in, leave cooking and come back to when it's time for the finale.

Preheat the oven to 210°C fan/230°C/450°F/Gas 8.

Rub the sweet potatoes with some oil and sea salt, then place on a large baking sheet. Bake on the top shelf in the preheated oven for 40 minutes.

Remove the sweet potatoes from the oven. Cut down the length of each one and open up, gently squishing the sides a little, to help create a well for the egg without ripping through to the base. Season the insides liberally and then sprinkle over the dried chilli/hot red pepper flakes. Return to the oven for a further 20 minutes, until the flesh is cooked through and soft.

Remove the baking sheet once more, and now that the flesh is even more malleable, use a spoon to gently mould an even more secure well in each one for the egg. Crack an egg into each well (don't worry if some of the white leaks out and onto the baking sheet).

Scatter the pumpkin seeds around the sweet potatoes and carefully return the baking sheet to the oven for 6–8 minutes (for a runny yolk). Transfer to plates and garnish with the toasty seeds, fresh coriander/cilantro and more dried chilli/hot red pepper flakes, if you like.

The eggs will continue to cook from the residual heat of the sweet potatoes, so make sure you serve immediately.

bacon & maple sesame bagels

A classic bacon and brown sauce sarnie is probably the most nostalgic and comforting meal for me. Crispy, glistening bacon from the AGA, brown sauce and melting butter loaded into squishy white bread. It's my desert island meal, all washed down with a brew (classy, I know). I have them when I'm tired, upset or ill, or when I just don't know what else to eat. It takes me right back to Saturday mornings as a child with my siblings. This bacon sarnie, however, is a bit different. Inspired by my time in America, where we lived when I was 12 years old; also, where we pre-teen Davies' discovered cream cheese and pancake houses.

1 teaspoon sesame seeds
6 rashers/slices smoked streaky
   bacon
2 bagels
1 tablespoon maple syrup
100 g/½ cup cream cheese
sea salt and freshly ground black
   pepper
vegetable oil, for frying

SERVES 2
TIME 15 minutes

Heat a large, non-stick frying pan/skillet over a medium heat and add the sesame seeds. Let them toast for 3–4 minutes until golden, then transfer to a small bowl and wipe out the pan.

Heat a small drizzle of oil in the pan on a medium-high heat and, once hot, add the bacon. Let it fry, turning occasionally until deep golden brown and crispy, approximately 7–10 minutes.

Meanwhile, halve and toast the bagels, then leave in the toaster to keep warm.

When the bacon is ready, remove from the heat and add the maple syrup and toasted sesame seeds to the pan. As the syrup sizzles, turn the bacon over a couple of times to coat.

Spread the cream cheese onto the bagels, sprinkle over a pinch of seasoning, top with the bacon. Serve immediately.

Swap ins
You can use any toasted bread instead of bagels, and runny honey instead of maple syrup. Back bacon is fine instead of streaky.

Leftovers
There shouldn't be any.

soda bread boulders

Soda bread has to be the easiest bread to make, whilst being wholesome and tasty too. These are boulders (roughly brought together and no time wasted on shaping perfectly) that you bake, cool, then freeze, ready to grab one or two, defrost and bake when you want. I've shared a couple of flavoured butter recipes alongside, also for the freezer. One of them was from my supper club and the other is a good 'odds and ends' butter mix.

200 g/1½ cups minus 1 tablespoon
  strong white bread flour, plus extra
  for dusting
200 g/1½ cups wholemeal plain/
  all-purpose flour
1 teaspoon sea salt
1 teaspoon bicarbonate of/baking
  soda
285 ml/1¼ cups buttermilk
  (or sour milk)

*a baking sheet, lined with
  parchment paper*

MAKES 8
TIME 35 minutes

Preheat the oven to 180°C fan/200°C/400°F/Gas 6.

Add all the dry ingredients to a large mixing bowl and mix to combine. Add the buttermilk and, using a metal spoon, combine, then tip out onto a clean work surface.

Briefly knead (it will be sticky) and then separate into eight balls. Pop all the soda bread boulders onto the lined baking sheet and with a knife dusted with flour, indent a cross into the centre of each boulder, to let the fairies out.

Bake on the middle shelf of the preheated oven for 23–25 minutes. Transfer to a cooling rack and cool down to room temperature. Once fully cool, place in a freezer bag and freeze.

When you want one (some), place on a baking sheet (with the oven back up at 180°C fan/ 200°C/400°F/Gas 6) and bake for 15 minutes until defrosted and golden brown. Enjoy with one of the butters. They're also great to mop up the Oxtail Casserole (see page 98) or Braised Short Rib (see page 94).

smoked salt, thyme & brown butter

8 sprigs fresh thyme
100 g/1 stick minus 1 tablespoon
  unsalted butter, at room
  temperature
1 teaspoon smoked salt
  (I use Dorset Salt Company)

MAKES 100 g/3½ oz.
TIME 15 minutes

Pull the thyme leaves from their stalks.

Add half the butter to a small saucepan over a medium heat with the thyme leaves and let melt, then bubble (swirling often) until you see lots of brown speckles and the butter has turned into a 'beurre noisette' (brown butter). You want good, brown colour in the pan, but also to avoid burning, so don't walk away. Once it's at beurre noisette stage, remove the pan from the heat, transfer to a bowl and cool down to a lukewarm temperature.

Once ready, gradually add the remaining room temperature butter, whisking constantly to combine. Once the butters and thyme have been incorporated together, add the salt and fold through. Taste to check the seasoning and remember the flavour will mellow slightly when cold, so don't be afraid to be bold!

Leave to cool, then roll into a log in some parchment paper and transfer to the freezer.

When you want some, just chop off a chunk and re-cover the exposed end, to avoid freezer burn. Return to the freezer and use again soon!

garlic & herb butter

2 garlic cloves
10 g/⅓ cup fresh herbs (parsley,
  coriander/cilantro, mint, tarragon)
100 g/1 stick minus 1 tablespoon
  unsalted butter, at room
  temperature

MAKES 100 g/3½ oz.
TIME 15 minutes

Peel and grate the garlic and finely chop the herbs (removing any hardy stalks).

Add a third of the butter to a small saucepan over a low heat and let the butter melt. Once melted, add the garlic, let it loosen and heat up into the melted butter for a minute.

Remove from the heat and then add to a heatproof bowl with the remaining butter, the herbs and a pinch of seasoning, mixing with a spoon to combine.

Once everything is incorporated, leave to cool, then roll into a log in some parchment paper and transfer to the freezer.

When you want some, just chop off a chunk and re-cover the exposed end with parchment paper. Return to the freezer and use again soon!

Swap ins

Try out different flavourings for the butters, and standard sea salt instead of the smoked salt is fine, just halve the amount and taste before freezing.

Leftovers

These recipes have been created to keep in the freezer, so it should be easy to use them up as and when you need.

indian scrambled eggs with naan or toast

My friend Ivan taught me this recipe having come back from a year working as a Naturalist Guide at Kipling Camp in the Kanha Tiger Reserve, Madhya Pradesh (home of the Jungle Book). The head chef at Kipling Camp, who has worked there for 30 years and who taught Ivan this recipe, serves the 'anda bhurji' in a roll as a picnic breakfast for guests, ahead of a day on safari. I, however, first tried them in Surrey. Although the surroundings weren't 'quite' as exotic as their origin, I loved the recipe and have been making them ever since. I serve them on toast, or sometimes naan bread, with tamarind chutney on the side.

Swap ins
Any type of onion will do and use any fresh tomatoes you have, you just need about 130–150 g/4½–5½ oz. fresh tomato. Ground cumin works instead of seeds.

Leftovers
This recipe serves 2 people so there shouldn't be much left, but you could cook basmati rice, then add to a frying pan/skillet with the leftover scrambled eggs and make an Indian-style egg-fried rice, with extra dried chilli/hot red pepper flakes and coriander/cilantro. Make sure the eggs and rice are piping hot.

olive oil or ghee, for cooking
1 onion, finely chopped
4 eggs
1 teaspoon cumin seeds
1 teaspoon ground turmeric
1 garlic clove, grated
2 vine tomatoes, roughly chopped
10 g/⅓ cup freshly chopped coriander/cilantro
sea salt and freshly ground black pepper
2 naans or slices of toast, to serve
dried chilli/hot red pepper flakes, to serve
tamarind chutney, to serve (optional)

SERVES 2
TIME 15 minutes

Heat a generous glug of oil or a large knob/pat of ghee in a medium, non-stick frying pan/skillet on a medium-high heat and when hot, add the chopped onion. Let sizzle and soften for 5 minutes.

Whisk the eggs in a bowl with a fork, then set aside.

Once the onions have had 5 minutes, add the cumin seeds and turmeric. Cook for a further minute, then add the garlic and chopped tomatoes. Stir to combine well and cook for a further minute.

Remove the pan from the heat briefly, add the eggs, mixing well, then return to the heat again and scramble for a final minute or two.

Once the eggs are ready, remove from the heat and fold through the coriander/cilantro and season.

Serve on warmed naans or toast, generously sprinkle over some dried chilli/hot red pepper flakes and a spoonful of tamarind chutney on the side, if you have some.

'not-too sweet' bircher muesli

1 pear, cored
1 large apple, cored
200 g/1½ cups porridge oats
250 ml/1 cup plus 1 tablespoon whole
    milk (cow's, oat, soy or coconut)
60 ml/¼ cup apple juice
2 tablespoons golden caster/
    superfine or granulated sugar
    (or maple syrup)
50 g/1¾ oz. sultanas
50 g/1¾ oz. cashews
fresh or cooked fruit, to serve

SERVES 4–6
TIME 10 minutes, plus soaking
overnight

Bircher museli is a great breakfast to prep on a Sunday and have in the fridge for a few days, ready to enjoy as quickly as cereal, but so much more satisfying and tasty. It's also a go-to for me when I have people staying over. Make the pancakes with any leftover bircher mix you have for a weekend breakfast or sweet supper, if that takes your fancy one evening.

Grate the pear and apple into a mixing bowl, then add the oats, milk, juice, sugar, sultanas and cashews. Mix to combine and leave in the fridge overnight, covered.

Serve in the morning with plenty of fruit and an extra splash of milk, if you like.

Swap ins
So many options here. Play around with different milks, honey, agave or maple syrup instead of sugar, different dried fruits and nuts.

Leftovers
See opposite for a simple pancake recipe, using up leftover bircher muesli.

bircher pancakes

100 g/¾ cup self-raising/rising flour
200 g/1½ cups bircher muesli
  (see opposite)
60 ml/¼ cup whole milk
50 g/¼ cup natural/plain yogurt
2 teaspoons runny honey
50 g/1¾ oz. fresh berries (blueberries,
  raspberries) or pitted cherries
butter, for frying
extra honey, to serve
banana, yogurt, mixed nuts and
  seeds, to serve

MAKES 6
TIME 20 minutes

Add the flour to the leftover bircher muesli and mix to combine, then add the milk, yogurt, honey and berries. Fold the ingredients together to combine well.

Heat a non-stick frying pan/skillet over a medium heat and, once hot, add a knob/pat of butter to the pan. Let the butter melt and sizzle briefly.

Add a heaped dessertspoonful of the pancake mix to the pan and spread out to a diameter of 8–10 cm/ 3¼–4 inches. Let fry for 2 minutes, then flip and cook the other side until also golden and set, another minute or two.

Transfer to a plate and repeat with the remaining batter.

Serve with sliced banana, yogurt, a little extra honey and some mixed nuts or seeds.

Swap ins

You could use wholemeal/whole-wheat self-raising/rising flour and replace the milk and yogurt with dairy-free options of your choice. As always, use agave instead of honey... or even just some caster sugar. Play around with different berries in the pancake mix or try adding sliced banana.

Leftovers

This is a leftovers recipe, but store in an airtight container in the fridge for up to 1 day and serve up cold with ice cream and fruit, or just more yogurt as pudding.

ginger juice

This is a super easy fresh and zingy juice that is a great alternative to soft drinks. Make a jug/pitcher of it for brunch, add gin or vodka for homemade cocktails, or freeze into ice cubes (see leftovers advice), or just have in the fridge over the weekend ready to share.

50 g/1¾ oz. fresh ginger
800 ml/3⅓ cups water
juice from 1 lemon
juice from 1 lime
6 tablespoons runny honey or agave
5 ice cubes
ice cubes, to serve
fresh mint, to serve

MAKES 1 litre/quart
TIME 10 minutes

Peel the ginger and then add to a food processor with a splash of the measured water. Blitz the ginger and water to let the ginger break down, about 30 seconds–1 minute.

Add the lemon and lime juices to the food processor along with the honey, remaining water and the ice. Blitz for about a minute until very smooth. Serve in a jug/pitcher with plenty of ice and fresh mint.

Leftovers
Store in the fridge for up to 3 days or freeze the juice in an ice cube tray and serve the frozen cubes in water with some fresh herbs, as and when you like.

berry juice

This recipe is best made in the warmer months, when berries are in season, but you can also make it with frozen berries. Blitz up in a jug blender and store in the fridge for up to 2 days. Packed with vitamins, this is a great juice to pep you up.

juice of 1 orange
1 carrot
450 g/1 lb. mixed berries:
    strawberries, blueberries, pitted
    cherries, raspberries or blackberries
1 tablespoon berry jam/jelly
250 ml/1 cup plus 1 tablespoon water
ice cubes, to serve

MAKES 1 litre/quart
TIME 5 minutes

Juice the orange and grate the carrot.

Add all the ingredients, except the water, to a jug-blender (or even better use a NutriBullet). Blitz to break down the fruit and combine, then add the water and blitz again. Pour into glasses with plenty of ice to serve. Store in the fridge for up to 2 days or freeze for up to 1 month.

Swap ins
You can use honey, agave syrup or sugar as the sweetener, and replace the carrot with a banana if you would like a more smoothie-like consistency.

sweet ginger tea

I was first given this tea by my Indian neighbour; it was so warming I only drank tea like it for a week after. Ginger aids digestion and the honey offers some sweet satisfaction, perfect for post-meal cravings.

60 g/2¼ oz. fresh ginger, peeled and roughly chopped
2 black tea bags
milk, to serve
runny honey, to serve

SERVES 4
TIME 10 minutes

Put the ginger into a saucepan with 1 litre/quart water and the tea bags, then bring to the boil. Once boiling, remove the pan from the heat and stand for a minute before straining into tea cups, with a dash of milk and a drop or two of honey.

Swap ins
Very simple swap ins would be loose black tea (probably more authentic, too, I just use tea bags as I always have them in my cupboard) and then sugar as a replacement for honey.

Leftovers
Cool down and serve chilled as an iced tea, topped up with cold water, fresh chunks of ginger, lemon slices and lots of ice (no milk).

spiced mint tea

This is a wonderfully soothing refreshment for after dinner, first thing in the morning or as and when you feel like it! It's also lovely chilled and served over ice, so don't pour away the teapot dregs!

1 litre/quart boiling water
3 cardamom pods, bashed
10 g/⅓ oz. fresh mint
2 cloves
2 star anise

SERVES 4
TIME 5 minutes

Fill a teapot with hot water to warm.
Pour out the warming water from the teapot, fill with the measured fresh boiling water and add all the remaining ingredients. Let the tea stand for 5 minutes before straining and serving.

Swap ins
You could make this tea without any of the spices above and it would still be lovely, so if you don't have it all, just make do with what you have.

Leftovers
Cool to room temperature, strain and then freeze into ice cubes. Add an iced tea cube to a mug with boiling water and you have the same tea without any ingredients needed. That, or add the ice cubes to water, gin or vodka tonics for a minty, spiced hint as the ice melts.

lunch to bed

Simple, savoury meals for lunch and later, mid-week or weekend, from quick-fix suppers to storecupboard raids. Best for (but not bound to) serving 2–4 people.

carrot, coriander & caraway soup

Caraway is one of my favourite spices, I adore it in both sweet and savoury dishes. You'll find it in the hazelnut brittle (see page 138), but here it's paired with the classic carrot and coriander.

1 onion, finely chopped
4 garlic cloves, grated
1 tablespoon coriander seeds, crushed
1 tablespoon caraway seeds
650 g/23 oz. carrots, cut into 1-cm/
    ⅜-inch slices
1.5 litres/6 cups plus 4 tablespoons
    vegetable stock
sea salt and freshly ground black
    pepper
oil, for cooking
20 g/¾ oz. freshly chopped coriander/
    cilantro, plus extra leaves, to serve

FOR THE CROUTONS
2–3 slices bread (whatever you've got)
1 tablespoon olive oil
20 g/¾ oz. hard cheese (any)

SERVES 4
TIME 50 minutes

Swap ins
You can use fennel seeds instead of caraway seeds, and cumin seeds instead of coriander seeds. Use fresh parsley instead of fresh coriander/cilantro.

Leftovers
Freeze any leftover soup once it has fully cooled, and defrost within a month of doing so. Whip up the Soda Bread Boulders (see page 32) to serve.

Preheat the oven to 200°C fan/220°C/425°F/Gas 7.

Heat a generous glug of oil in a large saucepan or casserole and, once hot, add the onion. Sweat for 5 minutes. Next, add the garlic, coriander seeds and caraway seeds. Fry for 1 minute, until fragrant, then add the carrots. Fry for 5 minutes, stirring often, then add the vegetable stock.

Bring the soup to the boil, then immediately reduce to a simmer. Leave on the hob/stovetop gently bubbling away for 20 minutes.

Meanwhile, tear up the bread into croutons, place on a baking sheet, drizzle with the olive oil and grate over the cheese. Place on the top shelf of the preheated oven and bake until golden and the cheese has melted, about 10 minutes.

Blitz the soup with a stick blender, taste, season and taste again. Add the fresh coriander/cilantro, then briefly blitz again. Transfer to bowls and top with the croutons, and some extra coriander/cilantro, if you like.

miso mushrooms
on toast

Miso paste has probiotic properties, so it's great for our immune system, digestion and gut and it's incredibly moreish too. I've used miso paste in the aubergine/eggplant recipe on page 71, so you could cook that with the leftover miso paste (or vice versa), but once opened it lives in the fridge, so you'll be fine to leave it there (follow instructions on the jar).

**2 slices bread (I use spelt and rye
   sourdough)**
1 lemon
**400 g/14 oz. mixed mushrooms
   (I use shiitake and chestnut), sliced**
2 large garlic cloves, grated
50 g/1¾ oz. red miso paste
30 ml/2 tablespoons water (a splash)
1 teaspoon sesame oil
10 g/⅓ oz. freshly chopped parsley
**sea salt and freshly ground black
   pepper**
olive oil, for cooking
salad or greens, to serve

SERVES 2
TIME 15 minutes

Toast the bread (leaving it in the toaster to keep warm) and cut the lemon in half.

Heat a drizzle of oil in a large frying pan/skillet and, once hot, add the mushrooms. Pan-fry for 7–10 minutes, tossing occasionally, until well-browned and tender, but not overcooked.

Next, add the garlic, miso paste, a good squeeze of lemon juice, water and sesame oil and let sizzle, tossing to coat the mushrooms. Fry for a minute or two, then remove from the heat, add the parsley, and fold through. Taste to check for seasoning, then pile on top of toast and serve with salad or greens on the side. Chop up the leftover lemon and pop a wedge on each plate.

Swap ins
You can use any mushrooms here, but slice any large ones to about the size of a cherry tomato. White miso paste is great too. Replace the parsley with fresh coriander/cilantro, and if you don't have sesame oil, any nut oil will work.

Leftovers
Roughly chop up the leftover cooked mushrooms and throw them into a chilli con carne as it simmers away (it's just a good umami hit to add to the sauce), or serve chilled as a mushroom paté style snack on crackers with some fresh herbs.

crispy gnocchi with lemon, tomatoes, spinach & crème fraîche

You could, of course, make the gnocchi from scratch, but this is a quick-fix-meal recipe, with minimal faff and it uses just one pan. Gnocchi, in my opinion, should always be fried; I'm a sucker for that crispy crust and pillowy centre, so here's a recipe creating just that result, for your midweek meal repertoire.

500 g/1 lb. 2 oz. ready-made gnocchi
250 g/9 oz. mixed fresh tomatoes:
    cherry, vine and/or plum
2 garlic cloves, grated
200 g/7 oz. spinach
150 ml/⅔ cup crème fraîche
1 lemon
50 ml/3½ tablespoons boiling water
sea salt and freshly ground black
    pepper
vegetable oil, for frying
80 g/3 oz. rocket/arugula, to serve
olive oil, to serve

SERVES 4
TIME 20 minutes

Swap ins
You need the gnocchi and fresh tomatoes for this recipe, but you could use garlic purée instead of fresh, kale to replace the spinach and soured/sour cream instead of crème fraîche.

Heat a good drizzle of vegetable oil in a large, non-stick frying pan/skillet over a medium-high heat and when hot, add the gnocchi. Fry, tossing every minute, for 8–10 minutes.

Halve the cherry tomatoes and roughly chop any larger tomatoes.

Once the gnocchi is golden-brown and crispy, reduce the heat slightly and add the garlic and tomatoes to the pan. Sizzle gently for 2 minutes, then add half of the spinach and wilt for a minute, followed by the remaining spinach, letting it also wilt, and fold all the ingredients together. Finally, add the crème fraîche, a good squeeze of lemon juice and the boiling water.

Let the sauce come to the boil, then remove from the heat. Stir well, taste to check for seasoning, then pile into bowls. Serve with some rocket/arugula on the side and use the remaining lemon and some olive oil to drizzle over the top.

Leftovers
Simply reheat this dish (until piping hot) with an extra splash of water, with some fresh lemon juice and fresh tomatoes to bulk it out again. The spinach won't look or taste quite as fresh.

garlic & herb pasta

This is a simple pasta recipe with a hearty amount of roasted garlic, plenty of fresh herbs, Parmesan and an egg yolk binding it all together at the end. Serve up 'à deux', or scale up (by doubling the ingredients) and make a big bowl of the stuff. Double date?

2 garlic bulbs
1 tablespoon olive oil, plus extra
    for frying
220 g/8 oz. dried tagliatelle
1 shallot, finely chopped
1 vegetable stock gel cube/stock pot
10 g/⅓ oz. freshly chopped parsley
50 g/1¾ oz. Parmesan, grated
2 egg yolks
sea salt and freshly ground black
    pepper
lemon wedges, to serve (optional)

*baking sheet, lined with aluminium
    foil*

SERVES 2
TIME 40 minutes

Swap ins
You can use spaghetti or fettuccine instead of tagliatelle, hard Italian cheese instead of Parmesan and coriander/cilantro instead of parsley.

Leftovers
Serve as a pasta salad, just add a drizzle of olive oil and a handful of rocket/arugula. Use unused egg whites in a pavlova (see page 138).

Preheat the oven to 170°C fan/190°C/375°F/Gas 5.

Halve the garlic bulbs through the equator and put onto the prepared baking sheet with the cut-sides-facing down. Pour over the olive oil and add a pinch of sea salt. Seal up the foil around the garlic, transfer to the preheated oven and roast for 20 minutes. Remove the garlic from the oven, turn the halves over so the cut sides are facing up and roast for a further 10 minutes.

Meanwhile, bring a large pan of salted water to the boil and, once bubbling, add the pasta and boil according to package instructions, minus 2 minutes.

Heat a large frying pan/skillet over a medium heat with a drizzle of olive oil and, once hot, add the shallot. Fry gently for 5 minutes until softening and starting to colour lightly, then turn the heat off and wait for the garlic to finish roasting.

When the pasta is ready, scoop up 200 ml/1 cup of the starchy pasta water for later, then drain, rinse and cool the pasta under cold water. Drizzle a little olive oil over the drained pasta to stop it sticking together and set aside in the colander.

When the garlic has had its time, remove from the oven, then squeeze out the roasted cloves from the skin transferring them to a board. Briefly and roughly mash them with the back of a spoon, then add them to the shallot in the pan.

Return the pan to a medium heat, add the reserved pasta water and stock gel/stock pot, bring to a simmer and gently bubble for a minute, stirring to dissolve the stock. Pile in the cooked pasta, parsley and almost all of the Parmesan. Stir and fold the ingredients into each other, and season, to taste.

Divide the pasta into bowls and then gently place a yolk into the centre of each bowl and sprinkle the remaining Parmesan on top. Serve immediately. Use your fork to fold the yolk through the pasta before digging in. Serve with wedges of lemon if you'd like a squeeze of juice.

tomato & beef risotto

2 beef stock cubes/stock pots
1 onion, finely chopped
10 g/⅓ oz. fresh basil
250 g/9 oz. mixed fresh tomatoes:
   cherry, vine and/or plum
2 garlic cloves, grated
350 g/12 oz. risotto rice
2 tablespoons tomato purée/paste
20 g/1½ tablespoons salted butter
30 g/1 oz. Parmesan, plus extra
   to serve
½ lemon
sea salt and freshly ground black
   pepper
olive oil, for cooking

SERVES 4
TIME 45 minutes

I made this recipe just before I started writing this book, when there wasn't much food in the house. I had beef stock jellies/stock pots, some risotto rice, half an onion and a few old tomatoes. I cooked it up and we wolfed it down. The beef stock gives a delicious richness to the meal, without it being overpowering or heavy. You almost don't need the Parmesan at the end, I just add some to the pan and then leave extra to serve if you want more.

Add 1.5 litres/6 cups plus 4 tablespoons water and the beef stock cubes to a saucepan and bring to the boil. Once boiling, reduce the heat to very low.

Add a good drizzle of olive oil to a wide-bottomed, non-stick saucepan and, once hot, add the onion. Let it sweat for 5 minutes, until softening.

Separate the basil leaves from their stalks, leaving the leaves whole and finely slicing the stalks. Halve any cherry tomatoes and roughly chop anything larger.

Once the onion has had 5 minutes, add the garlic and basil stalks and sizzle for a further minute. Add the rice and stir to coat in the oil, then add the tomato purée/paste, and stir constantly for 2 minutes.

Add the first ladleful of beef stock along with the prepared tomatoes and let the risotto gently bubble, stirring often. Once the liquid has almost completely been absorbed, add another ladleful of stock. Settle the temperature to a gentle simmer, and once that ladleful has almost completely absorbed, add a third. Continue with this process until the risotto rice is almost al dente. It should take about 20 minutes.

When the rice is almost ready, season, taste, season again and add a final, scant ladleful of stock. Stir well.

Remove the risotto from the heat and add the butter and basil leaves, then grate in the Parmesan and add a squeeze of lemon juice.

Stir very well, then taste to check for seasoning one more time. Divide into bowls and serve with some extra Parmesan and a grater within arm's reach.

Swap ins

Chicken or vegetable stock is fine, but it's the beef stock that really gives this recipe its uniqueness. Parsley instead of basil is fine too.

Leftovers

Make arancini! Look that one up, it'll take too long for me to explain!

Swap ins

If you don't have any leftover salad, thinly slice a fresh fennel bulb and roast with some lemon juice, chives and dill and olive oil for 5–10 more minutes than stated in the method. If you don't have fresh tomatoes, use some passata. Use a leek instead of the onion.

lemon-roasted fennel
& dill pasta bake

Fennel and tomato go really well together, so this was a simple combination created to avoid wasting a perfectly good, albeit soggy, leftover salad (from page 107). I have added bacon lardons, but you can omit them.

FOR THE PASTA BAKE
200–300 g/7–10½ oz. leftover
  Raw Fennel, Chive & Dill Salad
  (see page 107)
400 g/14 oz. dried pasta, I use penne
  or fusilli
200 g/7 oz. smoked bacon lardons
1 onion, finely chopped
4 garlic cloves, grated
1 tablespoon tomato purée/paste
400 g/14 oz. fresh tomatoes: cherry,
  vine or plum, roughly chopped
400-g/14-oz. can chopped tomatoes
1 vegetable stock cube/stock pot

FOR THE TOPPING
5 g/⅛ oz. fresh thyme
50 g/1 cup panko breadcrumbs
3 tablespoons olive oil

sea salt and freshly ground black
  pepper
olive oil, for cooking
salad or vegetables, to serve

30 x 23 x 5 cm/11¾ x 9 x 2 inch
  baking dish

SERVES 4–6
TIME 1 hour

Leftovers
Reheat until piping hot and eat again!

Preheat the oven to 200°C fan/220°C/425°F/Gas 7.

Add the leftover fennel salad to a baking sheet with a small drizzle of olive oil and a pinch of seasoning, then bake in the preheated oven on the top shelf for 15 minutes, until coloured and shrunken.

Meanwhile, bring a large saucepan of salted water to the boil and cook the pasta according to the package instructions, minus 2 minutes. Drain and rinse the pasta in a colander, then return to the pan (off the heat) and set aside.

Add a drizzle of oil to a wide-bottomed saucepan and, once hot, add the bacon lardons. Fry for 5 minutes until golden. Add the onion to the pan. Cook for 5 minutes, stirring often, and once also golden, add the garlic and cook for a minute. Next, add the tomato purée/paste, stir well and cook for 1 minute more.

Add the fresh and canned tomatoes and vegetable stock cube/stock pot to the pan. Fill the empty tomato can one-third full with water and add that too. Bring the sauce to the boil, then reduce the heat and simmer for 10 minutes, stirring often.

Once the roasted fennel salad is ready, transfer it straight to the tomato sauce and be sure to scrape in any sticky bits from the baking sheet too.

Whilst the sauce simmers, prep the topping. Tear the thyme leaves up (removing the thickest stalks) and add to a bowl with the breadcrumbs, oil and a generous pinch of black pepper. Mix well to combine.

When ready, pour the tomato and fennel sauce over the cooked pasta. Mix well to combine, taste to check for seasoning once more and then transfer into the large baking dish.

Sprinkle the topping evenly over the pasta mixture and place on the top shelf in the oven. Bake for 20 minutes until the sauce is bubbling and the topping has crisped up. Serve with salad or vegetables.

roasted stuffed tomatoes, haddock & greens

4 skinless haddock fillets
 (about 130 g/4½ oz. each)
1 lemon, zested and cut into wedges
4 large vine tomatoes
2 garlic cloves, grated
10 g/⅓ oz. freshly chopped parsley
a few sprigs fresh oregano, chopped
2 canned anchovies, drained and
 roughly chopped
250 g/9 oz. spring greens
4 spring onions/scallions, thinly
 sliced
sea salt and freshly ground black
 pepper
olive oil, for cooking

SERVES 4
TIME 35 minutes

Swap ins
Skin-on is, of course, fine, swap haddock for smoked haddock, sustainable (MSC) cod, pollock or plaice. Spring greens for cavolo nero, spinach or Tenderstem broccoli.

Leftovers
Slice the stuffed tomatoes, break up the fish, then add everything to a small frying pan/skillet, heat until piping hot, make a couple of wells and crack an egg into each one. Cook until the whites are firm but the yolks still runny. Mop up with bread.

The roasted tomatoes are the main element of prep here, but it's still a super-quick and easy meal. Pop the tomatoes and fish on the same baking sheet to save on washing up, then it's just a quick fry for the greens. I've used spring greens with spring onions/scallions, but really, you can use whatever's handy.

Preheat the oven to 180°C fan/200°C/400°F/Gas 6.

Put the haddock fillets, lemon zest, some seasoning and a drizzle of oil onto a plate and gently roll the haddock fillets over a few times to coat. Set aside.

Slice the top off each tomato (stalk end, but don't throw away). Using a spoon, carefully scoop out the tomato flesh and put into a pestle and mortar (or bowl). Add the garlic, parsley, oregano and anchovies, then grind to break up and combine. Refill the tomatoes with the mixture and top with the reserved tomato lids. Put the tomatoes onto a large baking sheet. If they need help standing up, place one stuffed tomato in each corner of the baking sheet. Season and drizzle with a little oil, then transfer to the top shelf of the preheated oven and bake for 10 minutes.

Halve the spring greens lengthways, then thickly slice widthways and set aside.

Once the 10 minutes are up, add the fish to the baking sheet, pouring over any plate juices/oil, then return to the oven for 7–8 minutes, or until the fish is cooked through.

Finally, heat a drizzle of oil in a large frying pan/skillet over a medium-high heat and, once hot, add the spring onions/scallions and cook for a minute. Top with all of the spring greens and fry for 4 minutes, tossing often until wilted and slightly coloured. Season with some salt and pepper and a squeeze of lemon juice. Remove from the heat and divide onto plates.

Once out of the oven, divide the haddock and tomatoes between plates and serve immediately, with any remaining lemon wedges.

saucy coconut noodles with prawns

1 lemongrass stem
60 g/2¼ oz. fresh ginger, peeled
    and finely chopped
5 garlic cloves, grated
2 red chillies/chiles, finely chopped
3 tablespoons fish sauce
2 x 400-g/14-oz. cans coconut milk
600 ml/2½ cups vegetable stock
a pinch of granulated sugar
200 g/7 oz. greens: sugarsnap peas,
    edamame, green beans, babycorn
    or Tenderstem broccoli
200 g/7 oz. dried rice noodles
180 g/6¼ oz. peeled prawns/shrimp,
    peeled
2 limes, cut into halves
40 g/1½ oz. peanuts, roughly chopped
30 g/1 oz. freshly chopped coriander/
    cilantro
vegetable or coconut oil, for frying
sesame oil, to serve
roasted chilli/chili oil, to serve

SERVES 4
TIME 35 minutes

Swap ins

You can use ginger and garlic pastes
instead of the fresh stuff. Chicken stock is
fine instead of vegetable. Replace the rice
noodles with dried egg noodles (and cook
according to pack instructions). Have
whatever greens you like, and the
prawns/shrimp can be replaced with
leftover roast chicken (see page 88), fried
mini meatballs (see Thai Pork Burgers on
page 68), more veg or fried tofu. The
sugar can be any type of sugar too.

I went to my first ever cooking class at the age of 14. As well as all the foundations and basics, one of the recipes we learnt was Vietnamese Hotpot. It was so exotic and fragrant, like nothing I had eaten before. 15 years on and it's still a mid-week staple, the pan often plonked on the middle of the table. My recipe is inspired by that brilliant lesson by Diana and best served with something to wipe your chin!

Bash and halve the lemon grass.

Heat a generous drizzle of oil in a large saucepan over a medium-high heat, and, once hot, add the prepped ginger, garlic, chillies/chiles and lemongrass. Let fry for 3 minutes, then add the fish sauce and let bubble for 1 minute. Next, add the coconut milk, vegetable stock and a pinch of sugar.

Let the broth come to the boil, and then once bubbling, reduce the heat to a gentle simmer, and leave (stirring occasionally) for 15 minutes.

Meanwhile, prep the remaining ingredients. If you're using sugar snaps or green beans, halve them widthways, and if you're using tenderstem broccoli, cut into thirds widthways.

Once the broth has only got 5 minutes left to simmer, add the noodles. Let soften and briefly cook for 2 minutes, then add the vegetables and prawns/shrimp and let cook for the final 3 minutes. Add a good squeeze of lime and taste to check for seasoning.

Place the pan on the table with a ladle and tongs and serve into bowls. Top with the peanuts and coriander/cilantro and make sure you have the remaining lime wedges, some sesame oil, and roasted chilli oil on the side for anyone that wants it.

Leftovers

Reheat on the hob/stovetop, and serve once the broth and all the ingredients are piping hot. Fill out with some more cooked noodles and/or fresh vegetables.

fish & chips

This is a cover recipe to sort out your (or, at least, my) chip shop craving, without too much mess. You could make the chips from page 127, but this raw-to-roasted version works with any potato, is super simple and the timings work well with the fish.

700 g/25 oz. potatoes, cut into
   2–3-cm/¾–1¼-inch wedges
2 tablespoons vegetable oil
4 skinless pollock or coley fillets
finely grated zest and juice of 1 lemon
sea salt and freshly ground black
   pepper

FOR THE SAUCE
20 g/2 tablespoons capers, roughly
   chopped
150 ml/⅔ cup natural/plain yogurt
lemon juice (from above)

FOR THE LEMON CRUMB TOPPING
lemon zest (from above)
40 g/1½ oz. panko breadcrumbs
2 tablespoons olive oil, plus extra
   for cooking
cornichons, to serve

*large, non-stick, ovenproof frying
   pan/skillet*

SERVES 4
TIME 55 minutes

Swap ins

Use any potatoes that you have and haddock or cod is good in place of pollock. If you don't have capers, finely chop some extra cornichons and add those to the yogurt.

Preheat the oven to 210°C fan/230°C/450°F/Gas 8.

Put the potato wedges and vegetable oil into a large roasting pan, season and toss. Bake in the preheated oven for 50 minutes, turning halfway through cooking. When 10 minutes cooking time for the chips remains, reduce the temperature to 200°C fan/220°C/425°F/Gas 7.

For the sauce, put the capers and yogurt into a small bowl. Squeeze half of the zested lemon into the bowl. Add a pinch of seasoning and mix to combine.

For the topping, add the lemon zest to a bowl with the breadcrumbs and olive oil and mix. Heat the frying pan/skillet over a medium-high heat and when hot, add the breadcrumbs. Toast, tossing often, for 3–5 minutes until they turn a deep golden. Transfer back to the bowl and wipe out the pan (removing it from the heat first).

Heat a drizzle of olive oil in the frying pan/skillet and season both sides of the fish fillets. When the oil is hot, add the fish to the pan and fry for 2–3 minutes. Carefully turn the fillets over and spoon the toasted breadcrumbs on top of each fillet. Transfer the frying pan/skillet to the oven for 2–3 minutes, until the fish is cooked through and the breadcrumbs are hot. Serve with the sauce and cornichons on the side.

Leftovers

Reheat the potatoes in the oven until piping hot, and do the same with the fish. The sauce is great with anything, but particularly grilled meats.

chilli con carne parcels with spring onion, chive & soured cream

To be made in the aftermath of a chilli con carne evening, with the leftovers. Fold a can of cooked lentils through the chilli to bulk it out and make Cornish pasty-style parcels. Eat hot, with a dollop of leftover soured/sour cream for good measure.

300 g/10½ oz. leftover Chilli & Chocolate Con Carne (see page 101)
400-g/14-oz. can cooked lentils, rinsed and drained
10 g/⅓ oz. freshly chopped parsley
500 g/18 oz. ready-made puff pastry block
1 egg (or 45 ml/3 tablespoons milk)
plain/all-purpose flour, for dusting
sea salt and freshly ground black pepper
soured/sour cream, to serve
spring onions/scallions, to serve

2 baking sheets, lined with parchment paper

MAKES 4
TIME 1 hour, plus 30 minutes baking

Swap ins
Leftover bolognese or any meaty ragu would be great here. Make sure you taste to check for seasoning though. Parsley can be replaced with coriander/cilantro and milk instead of the egg wash.

Leftovers
This is a leftovers recipe, but by all means enjoy the leftovers of these cold, they're great for packed lunches and picnics. Use the spare pastry to make recipes on page 10.

Mix the chilli con carne with the lentils and parsley, and season to taste.

Dust the work surface and rolling pin liberally with flour. Roll out the puff pastry to about a 50 x 50 cm/ 20 x 20 inches square, then cut out four 15-cm/6-inch squares, or thereabouts. (See Leftovers note.)

Divide the chilli-lentil mixture onto one half of each square, popping each portion towards one corner of each square, but avoiding going too close to the edge.

Using a pastry brush, dab the whole rim/edge of one square with water, then fold the empty pastry half over the filling, to create a triangular parcel. Now using your fingers, press down along the layered edges of the parcel to seal and then transfer to one of the lined baking sheets. Repeat with the remaining squares.

Grab a fork and dip in the water, then go over your finger marks and press down gently to seal along the layered edges of the parcels. Transfer the baking sheets to the fridge and chill for at least 30 minutes.

Preheat the oven to 170°C fan/190°C/375°F/Gas 5.

Briefly beat the egg in a mug (or add the milk to a mug), then brush over all of the parcels. Transfer to the preheated oven and bake for 45 minutes until golden brown and the filling is piping hot. Swap the baking sheets over halfway through cooking so all of the parcels have a stint on the top shelf.

Don't worry if one or two of them burst slightly, it couldn't matter less.

Remove from the oven and leave to sit for a couple of minutes before eating. Serve with any leftover soured/sour cream and sliced spring onions/scallions.

thai pork burgers with pink onions & sesame cucumber

FOR THE PINK ONIONS
1 red onion
100 ml/⅓ cup plus 1 tablespoon
    white wine vinegar
½ teaspoon caster/granulated sugar

FOR THE PATTIES
10 g/⅓ oz. freshly chopped
    coriander/cilantro
40 g/1 ½ oz. fresh ginger, peeled
    and finely chopped
1 shallot, finely chopped
1 lemongrass stem, bashed,
    trimmed and finely chopped
2 garlic cloves, grated
30 g/1 oz. salted peanuts,
    roughly chopped
1 tablespoon fish sauce
1 tablespoon sesame oil
½ teaspoon dried chilli/hot red
    pepper flakes
600 g/21 oz. minced/ground pork

FOR THE SESAME CUCUMBER
½ cucumber
1 lime
1 tablespoon sesame seeds

FOR THE BUNS
10 g/⅓ oz. fresh mint
10 g/⅓ oz. fresh Thai basil
4 brioche buns, halved
30 g/1 oz. crispy onions
mayonnaise, to serve

sea salt and freshly ground black
    pepper
vegetable oil, for frying

SERVES 4
TIME 50 minutes

Whilst I want to avoid giving you shopping lists the size of my arm, this recipe is well worth its extended ingredients quantity. I'd advise making this meal in close proximity to cooking the Saucy Coconut Noodles with Prawns (see page 63), or Asian Chicken Salad (see page 92), to avoid wastage. I hope you love these burgers as much as I do!

Preheat the oven to 210°C fan/230°C/450°F/Gas 8.

Peel and thinly slice the red onion, add to a bowl with the white wine vinegar and sugar, then leave to pickle.

Prep all the ingredients for the burger patties: Hold the bunch of coriander/cilantro in your hand and break in half where the leaves start to grow. Finely chop the stalks and leave the leaves whole.

Put all the burger patty ingredients (apart from the coriander/cilantro leaves) into a large mixing bowl and mix with your hands for a minute. Shape into four patties, each about 2 cm/¾ inch thick and set aside on a plate.

Peel the cucumber into ribbons, then finely zest the lime. Add the ribbons, sesame seeds and lime juice (save the zest) to a bowl, mix to coat the ribbons and set aside.

Separate the mint and Thai basil leaves from their stalks, then add the leaves, along with the coriander/cilantro leaves, to a small bowl. Mix to combine and set aside.

Heat a drizzle of vegetable oil in a non-stick frying pan/skillet over a high heat and, once hot, add the burger patties. Cook for 5 minutes on each side (reduce the heat slightly if they start to burn), until well browned. Next, transfer to the oven (in the frying pan/skillet, if it's ovenproof, or on a small baking sheet). Let the burgers finish cooking in the oven for 2–3 minutes, or until cooked through. Add the brioche buns to the oven on the middle shelf at the same time, to toast.

Remove the burgers and buns from the oven and let the burgers rest for a couple of minutes. Meanwhile, spread the mayo on the base of the buns, top with the reserved lime zest, add some sesame cucumber, followed by the burgers, the herb mix, pink onions and some crispy onions. Add the bun lids and devour!

Swap ins

You could use minced/ground beef instead of the pork. You can use half an onion instead of the shallot, pastes instead of fresh ginger or garlic and cashews instead of peanuts. Use courgette/zucchini instead of cucumber and red wine vinegar or cider vinegar for the white wine vinegar. Swap in parsley for any of the fresh herbs.

Leftovers

Roll the (uncooked) burger patty mix into mini meatballs, pan-fry and add to the Saucy Coconut Noodles with Prawns, or make sausage rolls with some puff pastry. Keep the pink onions (for up to a week) and sesame cucumber (for up to 2 days) separately, in sealed containers in the fridge, and serve in sandwiches, on some buttered rye toast as a snack or even served on the side with curries or in salads.

honey, miso & soy aubergine, with yogurt & coriander

4 aubergines/eggplants
4 tablespoons runny honey
100 g/6 tablespoons red miso paste
3 tablespoons soy sauce
3 tablespoons vegetable oil
300 g/1⅓ cups natural/plain yogurt
30 g/1 oz. freshly chopped coriander/
  cilantro
1 fresh red chilli/chile, thinly sliced
30 g/1 oz. crispy onions
1 teaspoon pul biber
sea salt and freshly ground black
  pepper

*large baking sheet lined with
  parchment paper*

SERVES 4–6
TIME 70 minutes

Swap ins
Maple syrup for the honey is fine, then
the coriander/cilantro can be swapped
for parsley and the pul biber can be
swapped in for dried chilli/hot red
pepper flakes.

Leftovers
These are best reheated and served as
they are. Not very inventive, but it's true.
That, or chop up and fold the whole lot
through some cooked-and-cooled pasta
for a pasta salad. Delicious!

I created this recipe when I had a big group of
girlfriends to feed; almost half of them being
vegetarians. It was served in a massive dish with
serving spoons for everyone to help themselves,
but would also work wonderfully as a plated dish.
The key to this dish is cooking the aubergines/
eggplants for a long time (like all aubergine/eggplant
recipes, I feel). I'd also suggest serving with some
Little Gem lettuce and cucumber, it's rich and punchy
so pairs well with a refreshing leaf on the side.
That, or my fennel salad (see page 107).

Preheat the oven to 180°C fan/200°C/400°F/Gas 6.

Quarter the aubergines/eggplants lengthways and
put onto the prepared baking sheet. Add the honey,
miso paste, soy sauce and vegetable oil to a bowl with
some black pepper and mix with a fork to combine,
then pour liberally over the aubergines/eggplants and
rub into the wedges with your hands.

Place the dressed aubergines/eggplants on the top
shelf of the preheated oven and bake for 1 hour, turning
and basting 3 times. If the aubergines/eggplants colour
too much, cover with an upside-down baking sheet.
You want them to get a deep caramelization though,
so fear not.

Meanwhile, season the yogurt with a pinch of salt
and pepper and spread over a large serving dish.

Once the aubergines/eggplants are very soft, sticky
and well-coloured, transfer to the serving dish in a pile
on top of the yogurt, top with the coriander/cilantro,
crispy onions and fresh chilli/chile, finishing with the
pul biber. Make sure you spoon over any remaining
roasting sauce onto the dish as well.

suppers
for sharing

Wholesome, uncomplicated, feasting food; these recipes are best served in their cooking vessel or a big dish, carried straight to the table, ready for everyone to pile in. Minimal washing up and prep makes these recipes perfect for entertaining.

mac 'n' cheese
with greens

This is brilliant for feeding the masses. It's
filling, comforting and all baked in one dish.
You can add extras, such as spinach or onions.
I've piled leafy broccoli on top of the bake so
you don't need to wash up another vessel.

400 g/14 oz. dried macaroni
30 g/1 oz. fresh basil, torn
3 spring onions/scallions, trimmed
    and finely sliced
1 teaspoon garlic granules
3 tablespoons Dijon mustard
2 tablespoons grainy mustard
100 g/3½ oz. mature Cheddar, grated
100 g/3½ oz. Parmesan, grated
60 g/½ stick butter
60 g/scant ½ cup plain/all-purpose flour
800 ml/3⅓ cups whole milk, chilled
180 g/6¼ oz. purple-sprouting broccoli
sea salt and freshly ground black pepper
olive oil, for drizzling
salad leaves, to serve

2-litre/quart baking dish

SERVES 4–6
TIME 1 hour

Swap ins
Use any pasta you like. Swap in parsley
or a medley of herbs for the basil. Shallots
instead of spring onions/scallions and try
different cheeses and greens.

Leftovers
Great simply reheated in the oven,
served up with fresh greens or salad.

Preheat the oven to 200°C fan/220°C/425°F/Gas 7.

Bring a large saucepan of salted water to the boil.
Add the macaroni and boil for 7 minutes. Drain, then
run under cold water, return to the pan and set aside.

Add the basil and spring onions/scallions to a bowl
with the garlic and both mustards and then add the
Cheddar and 75 g/2¾ oz. of the Parmesan. Set aside.

To make a roux, melt the butter in a medium
saucepan and, once melted, bubble for 30 seconds.
Add the flour to the pan and mix well for 2 minutes,
letting the flour 'cook out' over a medium heat, but
avoid browning. Add a splash of the chilled milk to the
pan and mix well. When the milk has been absorbed,
add another splash and then continue the process a
few times over. Once the roux is loose, having added
a good few sloshes of milk, add the remaining milk and
continue to stir over a low heat until a thick sauce has
developed. It might feel like the sauce isn't going to
thicken, but it will, so persevere. It should take about
5 minutes once all the milk has been added.

Once the sauce has become thick, remove from the
heat and add the mustards, garlic, basil, spring onions/
scallions, cheeses and some black pepper.

Mix well to combine and adjust the seasoning
to taste. Pour the sauce over the macaroni and mix to
well combine. Transfer to the baking dish and sprinkle
over the remaining Parmesan. Put on the top shelf
of the preheated oven and bake for 20 minutes, until
golden and bubbling.

Meanwhile, halve any thick broccoli stems
lengthways, add to a mixing bowl and toss in a little
olive oil and seasoning.

Remove the mac 'n' cheese from the oven, put the
broccoli on top of the bake, in a fanning circle or, if your
vessel is square, just lay them out in a single-layered
row. Return to the oven on the top shelf and bake for
a further 10 minutes. Serve immediately.

Swap ins

So many options here. Play around with spices (can be ground instead of seeds), use potatoes or squash instead of sweet potato and 2 x 400-g/14-oz. cans of tomatoes.

Leftovers

Reheat the curry until piping hot. It's great folded into a frittata or served with baked potatoes.

roasted onion, mixed tomato & chickpea curry

This is one of my favourite curries to make when the fridge is looking a bit bare, but I want something wholesome, packed with goodness and flavour.

1 garlic bulb
2 red onions, skin on, cut into wedges
1 tablespoon coriander seeds
1 tablespoon mustard seeds
1 tablespoon ground turmeric
1 tablespoon ground ginger
1 cinnamon stick
2 tablespoons medium curry powder
1 onion, thinly sliced
1 carrot, finely chopped
1 celery stick/stalk, finely chopped
1 sweet potato, chopped into
   2–3-cm/¾–1¼-inch chunks
600 g/21 oz. mixed fresh tomatoes,
   roughly chopped
100 ml/⅓ cup plus 1 tablespoon
   boiling water
1 vegetable stock cube/stock pot
2 x 400-g/14-oz. cans chickpeas
200 g/7 oz. spinach
sea salt and freshly ground black
   pepper
vegetable oil, for roasting

FOR THE COCONUT RAITA
½ cucumber (approx. 160 g/5¾ oz.)
130 ml/½ cup coconut yogurt
grated zest and juice of 1 lime
1 garlic clove, peeled
basmati rice and canned lentils,
   to serve

SERVES 4
TIME 1½ hours

Preheat the oven to 200°C fan/220°C/425°F/Gas 7.

Break up the garlic bulb and put onto a baking sheet with the onion wedges. Drizzle with vegetable oil, season and toss to coat. Roast in the preheated oven for 25 minutes, until roasted and coloured.

Meanwhile, roughly crush the coriander seeds in a pestle and mortar. Heat a small frying pan/skillet over a medium heat, add the mustard seeds and crushed coriander seeds to the pan and toast for a couple of minutes, until fragrant. Remove from the heat and transfer to a small bowl. Add the remaining spices.

Heat a glug of vegetable oil in a large saucepan or casserole over a medium heat and, once hot, add the onion. Fry for 10 minutes until tender and starting to lightly caramelize. Add the carrot, celery and sweet potato to the pan along with the spices. Cook for 5 minutes, stirring often.

Once the red onions and garlic are ready, remove from the oven. Tear away the onion skins, and pull the garlic flesh from their skins too. Briefly mash the garlic flesh. Add the roasted onions and garlic to the curry.

Next, add the tomatoes, boiling water, stock cube or pot, chickpeas and chickpea water from the cans to the pan and bring to the boil. Reduce the heat and simmer for 45 minutes, stirring often.

To make the raita, grate the cucumber into a bowl, then add the yogurt and lime zest and juice, grate in the garlic clove and add a pinch of seasoning to the bowl. Mix well to combine and season to taste.

When the curry is a couple of minutes away from being ready, add the spinach and mix well to submerge and let wilt. Taste the curry, season generously and taste again.

Serve with cooked hot rice, lentils and the raita.

roasted mixed squash with almonds & tarragon

This recipe was the vegetarian and vegan main course option at my Home Bird supper club, from which this book has been developed. I could quite happily eat this meal every day – the mix of earthy, sweet, fresh and tangy flavours with multiple textures makes it a real winner.

8 small mixed squash, chopped
    into 5-cm/2-inch thick wedges
    (no need to peel or remove seeds)
8 tablespoons olive oil
2 tablespoons good-quality balsamic
    vinegar
80 g/1 cup flaked/slivered almonds
10 g/⅓ oz. fresh parsley
20 g/¾ oz. fresh tarragon
2 tablespoons maple syrup
2 tablespoons nigella seeds
sea salt and freshly ground black
    pepper

SERVES 6–8
TIME 55 minutes

Swap ins

Small mixed squash can be replaced with 2 butternut squashes cut into chunks, or any sweet pumpkin. Delicia pumpkin is amazing. Replace the almonds for whole almonds, hazelnuts or walnuts and the tarragon and parsley for coriander/cilantro, mint or basil.

Preheat the oven to 200°C fan/220°C/425°F/Gas 7.

Put the chopped squash onto two large baking sheets. Top the squash with half the olive oil, the balsamic vinegar and some seasoning, then toss well to coat. Roast on the top shelf of the oven for 50 minutes, turning halfway through.

Meanwhile, toast the almonds in a large frying pan/skillet on a medium heat for 3–4 minutes, tossing often. Once golden, transfer to a bowl and leave to cool. Roughly chop the parsley (and stalks) and tarragon (removing the stalk bases).

Make the salsa by mixing the almonds, herbs, remaining olive oil and a pinch of seasoning together.

Once the squash flesh is tender and sticky, transfer to a large dish, drizzle the maple syrup over the top, then pile on the salsa and finish with a generous sprinkling of nigella seeds.

Leftovers
Add into a frittata base
mix (see page 18) or make a
sandwich with some halloumi
or feta cheese and salad.

Swap ins

The ingredients used lend
themselves best to the
traditional bouillabaise dish,
but swap in onion, spring onion/
scallion or carrot ribbons instead
of leek and fennel if needed and
any type of tomato is fine. Use
white wine vinegar or just water
if you don't want to use wine.

Provence salmon parcels

Here, I've taken the flavours of bouillabaise, simplified them and popped into parcels. One pan, one baking dish, one small bowl and you're good to go. The flavours remind me of cooking school, enjoyed now without the stress and a glass of chilled white.

FOR THE SALMON PARCELS
1 leek, trimmed and finely sliced
1 fennel bulb, trimmed and finely
   sliced
1 garlic clove, grated
a pinch of saffron threads
1 beef tomato, halved and thinly sliced
6 strips of orange peel
4 skin-on salmon fillets
10 g/⅓ oz. fresh parsley
100 ml/⅓ cup white wine

FOR THE CHEAT'S ROUILLE
65 g/¼ cup mayonnaise
a pinch of saffron
1 teaspoon olive oil
1 garlic clove, grated
1 lemon

sea salt and freshly ground black
   pepper
olive oil, for frying

SERVES 4
TIME 30 minutes

Leftovers
Serve up cold with salad. Try with the Blackened Romano Pepper, Tomato & Chilli Salad (page 108), Dill & Basil Rice (page 124) and the Coriander & Black Onion Slaw (page 118).

Preheat the oven to 180°C fan/200°C/400°F/Gas 6.

Heat a drizzle of olive oil in a large frying pan/skillet on a medium heat and, once hot, add the sliced leek and fennel. Sweat, stirring often, for 10 minutes. Add the garlic and cook for a further minute, then remove from the heat. Add the pinch of saffron and mix to combine.

Put two large pieces of parchment paper, about 40.5-cm/16-inch square each, onto a clean work surface. Divide the sliced tomato between each piece, placing it in the centre, in a rough square shape (you are going to place the salmon on top, so make a bed for 2 fillets per piece of paper). Add the orange peel.

Next, divide the fennel and leek over the tomato. Add two raw salmon fillets to each open parcel, skin-side down, and tear the parsley over the top.

Season with salt and pepper and then bring the edges of the paper together, rolling the edges over and pinching tightly to seal. Before you finish the seal on each parcel, pour the wine into the openings, dividing it evenly. Seal the final section of the parcels, transfer to a baking sheet, then place on the top shelf of the oven.

Bake for 8–12 minutes, depending on how you like your salmon cooked. (For more well-done fillets, bake for 12 minutes.)

Meanwhile, make the cheat's rouille. Add the mayonnaise, saffron and olive oil to a bowl. Add the garlic followed by the lemon zest – grate half of the zest in. Mix well with a small pinch of seasoning and taste. Add a squeeze of lemon juice if it needs it.

Remove the parcels from the oven and carefully transfer the sealed parcels to a serving plate. Take to the table and enjoy opening the parcels together. Divide between plates and add a dollop of 'rouille' on the side. If you have some leftover lemon, cut it into wedges to serve.

veggie stew with tarragon dumplings

A golden vegetable stew with plenty of sweetness from the squash and apricots. Make the casserole a day in advance and whip up the dumplings when you're almost ready to serve. This one's for you, Mumma.

1 butternut squash, trimmed and cut into 4-cm/1-inch chunks (keep the seeds)
1 large onion, chopped
6 garlic cloves, grated
100 g/3½ oz. dried apricots, halved
6 spring onions/scallions, trimmed and quartered
1 celery stalk, cut into 1-cm/⅜-inch pieces
10 g/⅓ oz. fresh rosemary
100 ml/⅓ cup plus 1 tablespoon white wine (reisling or sauvignon blanc)
1 litre/quart vegetable stock
150 g/5½ oz. pearl barley
2 bay leaves

FOR THE DUMPLINGS
150 g/1 cup plus 2 tablespoons wholemeal/whole-wheat self-raising/rising flour
10 g/⅓ oz. freshly chopped parsley
1 teaspoon sea salt
roasted butternut squash seeds and any pulp from above
110 ml/⅓ cup plus 2 tablespoons buttermilk
sea salt and freshly ground black pepper
olive oil, for frying
crème fraîche, to serve

SERVES 4–6
TIME 1 hour 50 minutes

Preheat the oven to 200°C fan/220°C/425°F/Gas 7.

Put the squash onto a large baking sheet and add the seeds at one end. Drizzle with a little oil, season, then roast in the oven on the top shelf for 30 minutes.

Heat a large casserole dish with a drizzle of oil and, once hot, add the onion. Sweat for 5 minutes until beginning to soften. Add the garlic, apricots, spring onions/scallions, celery and rosemary. Cook for 2 minutes, stirring often, then deglaze with the white wine. Let the liquid bubble for about 30 seconds, then add the stock, pearl barley and bay leaves. Bring to the boil. Once boiling, reduce the heat to a simmer and let it very gently bubble away whilst you wait for the butternut squash to finish its 30 minutes of roasting.

As soon as it is ready, remove from the oven and add the squash chunks to the casserole. Reduce the oven to 170°C fan/190°C/375°F/Gas 5. Add a lid to the casserole and place in the oven for 45 minutes.

For the dumplings, add the flour, parsley, salt and roasted squash seeds (and pulp) to a bowl. Mix to combine, then add in the buttermilk. Bring together with a metal spoon, then turn out onto a clean work surface and briefly knead to bring together. Divide into six chunks, roll into six rough balls, place on a plate and pop in the fridge until needed, uncovered is fine.

When the stew has had its time, remove from the oven and taste to check for seasoning. Place the dumplings on top of the casserole. Return to the oven (without its lid) for 20 minutes until risen and golden. Let the casserole sit for 5 minutes before serving, then spoon into bowls, and serve with crème fraîche.

Swap ins
Any onion is fine, and use any pumpkin to replace the squash. Delicia pumpkin is amazing. Dates can be used instead of apricots and thyme instead of rosemary.

Leftovers
Blitz up the stew into a soup, or fold through some peas and cover with leftover pastry to make a pie.

braised chicken with citrus & greens

8 bone-in, skin-on chicken thighs
    and drumsticks (4 of each)
2 garlic bulbs, halved
2 red onions, cut into 3-cm/1¼-inch
    slices
1 celery stalk, cut into 3-cm/1¼-inch
    slices
2 tangerines, cut into 1-cm/⅜-inch
    slices
2 tablespoons plain/all-purpose flour
100 ml/⅓ cup plus 1 tablespoon
    white wine
1 chicken stock cube/stock pot
200 ml/scant 1 cup water
5 g/⅛ oz. fresh sage (about 2 sprigs)
10 g/⅓ oz. fresh rosemary
    (about 4 sprigs)
100 g/3½ oz. asparagus
    (or green beans, if not in season)
50 g/1¾ oz. peas (fresh or frozen)
sea salt and freshly ground black
    pepper
vegetable oil, for frying

SERVES 4–6
TIME 1 hour

....

Swap ins
Replace red onions with any onion and
the tangies with an orange. Use any hardy
herbs and whatever veg is in season.
Be conscious that the greens only get
braised for 10 minutes, so chop well.

Leftovers
This is lovely heated up in a pan and
served with a crunchy salad, best to cut
away the chicken from the bones and
heat until piping hot. You could also do
this, add more stock and blitz up into a
soup. The flavours are lovely.

One-pot meals are the best and there's something
unbeatable about vegetables being cooked with
bone-in chicken juices and stock. I really love this
recipe instead of a roast, when I want meat and
seasonal vegetables with a nourishing sauce.

Preheat the oven to 180°C fan/200°C/400°F/Gas 6.

Heat a generous glug of vegetable oil in a large
casserole. Season the chicken well and add to the
casserole (in batches), skin-side down, and fry until
browned, about 5–6 minutes. Once the chicken skin
has been browned, transfer to a plate and add the
shallots, garlic bulb halves, celery and tangerines to
the pan. Fry for 2 minutes on the same high heat, then
reduce slightly and fry gently for a further 3 minutes,
to start to soften and lightly colour.

Add the flour to the pan. Stir well to coat the
vegetables and fruit and cook it out for about
30 seconds. Next, pour the wine over the floured
ingredients and let it bubble and deglaze for a minute.

Add the chicken stock cube/stock pot, water, sage
and rosemary sprigs and some seasoning to the pan,
stir to combine all of the ingredients and bring to the
boil. Once boiling, remove from the heat and nestle
the browned chicken back in, skin-side up.

Transfer the casserole to the preheated oven and
bake for 35 minutes, until cooked through and all the
ingredients are tender.

Snap off any hardy ends of the asparagus stalks.
When there are only 10 minutes left of the cooking
time, add the peas to the pan, settling them into the
braising liquor, and add the asparagus too. Return
to the oven for the final 10 minutes.

Remove from the oven and leave to sit for a couple
of minutes before serving.

pork chops with baked chillies & pears

3 pears (I use Conference)
6 fresh red chillies/chiles
10 g/⅓ oz. fresh rosemary sprigs
2 tablespoons olive oil
6 x 250–300 g/9–10½ oz. pork chops
sea salt and freshly ground black
    pepper
vegetable oil, for frying

SERVES 6
TIME 35 minutes

Swap ins

You can use eating apples instead of pears, and sweet peppers instead of chillies/chiles, if you wish. Rosemary can be replaced with oregano or thyme too.

Leftovers

Slice up and serve piled up on some focaccia, or fold through blanched green beans, couscous and lamb's lettuce, as a pork, chilli/chile and pear salad. It's also really good sliced up and stuffed into a warm, crusty roll with mayonnaise. That's how I used up the leftovers whilst testing the recipe anyway!

Chops remind me of my late Grandfather, Alan, also known to all as Gandalph. Whenever I visited him, he would either make me a Full English or chops (lamb or pork) and mash, with plenty of peas and gravy. This is a simple recipe with minimal ingredients, but a lovely combination of sweetness from the pork and pears and flavoursome heat from the chillies/chiles. Serve with mash and peas, like Gandalph, or with Proper Oven Chips (see page 127) and greens.

Preheat the oven to 180°C fan/200°C/400°F/Gas 6.

Slice the pears into discs and then halve the chillies/chiles lengthways, removing the seeds (or keep them in if you like heat). Add the pears, chillies/chiles and rosemary stalks to a large baking dish and drizzle with the olive oil and a pinch of seasoning. Toss to coat, then put into the preheated oven on the top shelf for 20 minutes.

Meanwhile, heat a drizzle of vegetable oil in a large, non-stick frying pan/skillet. Season the pork chops then add half of them to the frying pan/skillet and fry, for about 3 minutes on each side, until golden brown.

To sear the fat, hold the chops up with tongs and fry for a minute, gently pressing down.

Transfer the first batch to a plate and repeat the browning process with the remaining chops.

Once the pears and chillies/chiles have had 20 minutes, remove from the oven and turn over the pear discs. Add the browned chops to the baking dish on top of the pears and chillies/chiles and return to the oven for 10 minutes, until the chops are cooked through.

Remove the baking dish from the oven, and let sit for a couple of minutes before serving.

the best roast chicken with pan pastry croutons

FOR THE CHICKEN
1½ onions
1 lemon
1 garlic bulb
3 carrots
1 whole, medium, organic chicken
   (1.5 kg/3 lb. 5 oz.)
10 g/⅓ oz. fresh thyme sprigs
10 g/⅓ oz. fresh rosemary
30 g/¼ stick salted butter,
   cut into chunks
3 tablespoons vegetable oil
2 croissants, or a chunk of bread

FOR THE QUICK GRAVY
½ onion
1 teaspoon vegetable oil
1 tablespoon plain/all-purpose flour
30 ml/2 tablespoons white wine
pan juices from the chicken
250 ml/1 cup plus 1 tablespoon
   boiling water

sea salt and freshly ground black
   pepper

SERVES 4–6
TIME 1 hour 40 minutes

When a roast chicken is good, BOY is it good. Succulent meat, crispy skin, the carving ritual a joy with juicy oysters as payment... what's not to love? This is my version, unashamedly and brilliantly enhanced from my training at Le Cordon Bleu, where I learnt the '3-turn' process. What a revelation it was. So, I can't take credit for that stroke of genius (thanks Anthony Boyd and all), but I can encourage you to try it out along with my croissant croutons. Use plain (even pan au raisin) croissants, or old bread lying around. You won't look back!

Preheat the oven to 200°C fan/220°C/425°F/Gas 7.

Quarter the onions (skin-on) and cut the lemon into wedges, break up the garlic bulb and quarter the carrots widthways. Add them all to a large roasting pan and prepare a space for the chicken in the centre. Transfer the chicken to the roasting pan and stuff one wedge of lemon into the cavity, along with all of the fresh herbs.

Find the end of the skin at the base of the chicken breasts and, using your fingertips, make space between the flesh and the skin, by gently pushing through, moving side to side. Stuff the chunks of butter under the skin (try to avoid tearing the skin).

Drizzle the oil over the bird and vegetables, followed by a generous sprinkling of seasoning. Turn the chicken onto its side, so it is lying on its right leg. Use a few onion wedges or carrot pieces to help nestle the bird in place, then transfer to the preheated oven and roast for 20 minutes (you'll be roasting the chicken for 1 hour in three sets of 20 minutes).

When the first 20 minutes are up, remove from the oven and turn the chicken over onto its other side, so it now lays on its left leg. Return to the oven and roast for another 20 minutes.

When the next 20 minutes are complete, remove from the oven for a final time. Turn the chicken to sit

on its back (breasts up) and baste well. Tear the croissants or bread over the vegetables and then give them a loose toss to coat in some of the oils and juice. Return to the oven and roast for a third and final 20 minutes.

Once the hour is up, check that the chicken is fully cooked (the juices should run clear from the cavity, or just cut in between the breast and leg and check the colour) and if so, remove. If not, give it more time, until fully cooked.

Transfer the chicken to a board to rest for 20 minutes and very loosely cover it with foil. Transfer the vegetables and croutons to a heat resistant serving dish. Turn the oven off, then place the dish in the oven to keep warm.

Meanwhile, make the gravy. Finely chop the onion. Heat the oil in a frying pan/skillet on a medium heat and sweat for 5 minutes until beginning to soften. Add the flour and mix with a wooden spoon for a minute, then pour in the wine. Let the wine bubble away and be sure to mix well to incorporate the flour fully. Next, pour the roasting juices into the pan, making sure you scrape in all of the sticky lumps too, then add the boiling water and bring to the boil. Once bubbling, reduce the heat and simmer for 10–15 minutes. Season very well (taste and taste again) and add a pinch of sugar if it needs it.

Carve the chicken and transfer to the warm serving dish with the roasted veg and croutons. Serve with the gravy and your choice of accompaniments. I love greens, roast potatoes and a fresh crunchy green salad (see page 104).

Swap ins

Any root vegetables can go in the roasting pan, I like fennel, shallots, leeks, beetroot (beets) or cauliflower.

Leftovers

The chicken is perfect for Asian Chicken Salad (see page 92) and the roasted veg are great for frittatas (see page 18).

asian chicken salad

Communal living has its pros and cons, but I struck gold at the age of 23 and resided in bliss with four of my oldest friends. At the time, my friend, Kate, was working for a Thai restaurant start-up and would return from work with amazing ingredients, ideas and tips. This recipe was a 'Kate special' and became a comforting staple in our home. It's filled with wholesome, fragrant ingredients and, for me, loaded with nostalgia. I might add it was slightly different every time so it's the perfect fridge-raid meal too.

250 g/9 oz. basmati rice
4 eggs, at room temperature
1 small white cabbage (700 g/25 oz.)
1 carrot, coarsely grated
30 g/1 oz. freshly chopped coriander/ cilantro
5 spring onions/scallions, thinly sliced
1 red chilli/chile, thinly sliced
30 g/1 oz. fresh mint, stalks removed
3 limes
4 tablespoons fish sauce
4 tablespoons rice wine vinegar
2 tablespoons sesame oil
1 teaspoon soft light brown sugar
300–400 g/10½–14 oz. cooked chicken (preferably some dark meat, leftover from page 88)
50 g/1¾ oz. salted peanuts
sea salt and freshly ground black pepper

SERVES 6
TIME 25 minutes

Bring a large saucepan of water to the boil and, once boiling, add the rice and cook according to the package instructions (usually boiling for 8–12 minutes). Drain in a sieve/strainer and rinse in cold water.

Bring a small pan of water to the boil. Add the eggs and boil for 5 minutes (for a runny yolk). Drain the eggs and run under cold water until cool. Peel the eggs and set aside.

Meanwhile, halve the cabbage, then thinly slice each half widthways and shred. Add the cabbage, carrot, coriander/cilantro, spring onions/scallions, chilli/chile and mint leaves to a large salad bowl.

Next, halve all the limes and squeeze the juice from 3 halves into a small bowl. Add the fish sauce, rice wine vinegar, sesame oil, sugar and any leftover gravy from page 88. Mix to combine and set aside. Shred the cooked chicken using two forks and then halve the eggs.

When the rice is ready, add it to the salad bowl along with the chicken and the dressing and mix everything to combine. Finally, place the egg halves on top with a handful of peanuts and the remaining lime halves cut into wedges on the side. Season to taste.

Swap ins
Instead of chicken, try cooked pork, steak, prawns/shrimp or roasted aubergine/eggplant chunks. Try red instead of white cabbage, more coarsely grated carrot or Little Gem lettuce. Desiccated coconut is a great replacement (or addition) to the nuts.

Leftovers
It's best to eat them cold within 24 hours – top up with some more crunchy, raw veg.

braised short rib

2 red onions
2 carrots
2 celery stalks
2 garlic bulbs
1.65 kg/3⅔ lbs. short rib
   (about 5 short ribs)
2 tablespoons fennel seeds
3 tablespoons cumin seeds
2 tablespoons yellow mustard seeds
3 tablespoons Worcestershire sauce
2 tablespoons soy sauce
2 tablespoons ginger paste
2 tablespoons runny honey
2 tablespoons tomato purée/paste
4 bay leaves
1 bottle/750 ml red wine
   (I use a cabernet sauvignon)
1 litre/quart beef stock
20 g/¾ oz. fresh thyme sprigs
sea salt and freshly ground black
   pepper
vegetable oil, for frying

large ovenproof casserole/saucepan

SERVES 4
TIME 1 hour, plus 4 hours braising

This dish is definitely more suited to the winter months, or at least colder weather. I serve it with silky mashed potato and my Red Cos & Seed Salad (see page 110), however, it goes well with so many things. Just know that it is rich and the sauce is just as good as the meat, so you'll need something to mop it up with. I pretty much always make this dish a day in advance and then heat the whole thing up gently in a pan when it's time to eat. If you want to feed more than four, simply double up the recipe, but you'll need two casserole dishes.

Preheat the oven to 150°C fan/170°C/325°F/Gas 3.

Ask your butcher to prep the short rib, so they're about 12.5 cm/5 inches long each.

Peel, halve and cut the onions into thick wedges, cut the carrots widthways into thirds and quarter the celery stalks widthways. Halve the garlic bulbs through the centre/equator, leaving all the skin on.

Season the short rib all over, liberally.

Heat a drizzle of vegetable oil in a large frying pan/ skillet on a high heat. Once hot, brown all of the short rib pieces, on each side and ends very well, it should take about 15 minutes in total. If they don't all fit in one pan, do it in batches.

Meanwhile, heat another drizzle of oil in the large casserole/saucepan over a medium-high heat, and, once hot, add the onions, carrots and celery. Brown well too, for about 10 minutes. Don't be afraid of colour, you want the meat and vegetables to be well-browned.

Whilst everything colours, add the fennel, cumin and mustard seeds and garlic halves to a small bowl.

In a second bowl, add the Worcestershire sauce, soy, ginger, honey, tomato purée/paste and bay leaves.

Add the bowl of spices to the casserole, with the vegetables and fry for a minute (until fragrant), then add the second bowl of liquid ingredients and bubble for 30 seconds. Pour in the wine and beef stock, followed by the fresh thyme and browned short rib. Shuffle around the ingredients to settle the meat into the braising liquor and bring to the boil, then remove from the heat.

Scrunch up a large piece of parchment paper, then stretch out again, and place on top of the ingredients, finally sealing the casserole with a lid or foil. Place the casserole in the oven and braise for 4 hours.

Once cooked, carefully transfer the short rib to a serving dish, re-cover with the cartouche (parchment paper) and then some foil to keep warm. Next, pour the braising liquor through a fine sieve/strainer, catching the vegetables and spice seeds in the sieve/strainer (discard), and the liquid in a saucepan underneath. Scoop any excess oil off the surface with a ladle, then put the saucepan on a high heat and bring to the boil.

Let the sauce rapidly bubble down until it's thick, silky and rich, whilst keeping a spoon in a jug of hot water on the side, and skimming off any bubbly residue that clings to the edge of the pan, whilst it reduces. This should take about 15 minutes. Taste to check for seasoning (but it shouldn't need any), then pour over the short rib and serve.

NOTE If you are cooking this ahead of time, combine the reduced sauce and meat (you can now pull away the bones and discard) and heat it all up together in a pan until gently bubbling.

Swap ins

You want most of the ingredients I have included to get the flavour combinations intended, but feel free to try out other spices (and ground is absolutely fine, if you don't have the whole seeds).

Leftovers

The short rib is brilliant reheated (until piping hot) and enjoyed as it is, but it is also great in wraps, tacos, sarnies or used as a ragu with pasta.

oxtail casserole

1.5 kg/3 lb. 5 oz. oxtail
2 tablespoons plain/all-purpose
 flour
3 onions, thinly sliced
4 carrots, cut into quarters,
 widthways
2 celery stalks, cut into quarters,
 widthways
8 garlic cloves, grated
300 ml/1¼ cups red wine
500 g/1 lb. 2 oz. fresh plum
 tomatoes, quartered
1 can chopped tomatoes
1 litre/quart beef stock
5 g/⅛ oz. fresh thyme
5 g/⅛ oz. fresh oregano
3 bay leaves
500 g/1 lb. 2 oz. new potatoes
sea salt and freshly ground black
 pepper
vegetable oil, for frying

large casserole
kitchen string

SERVES 6–8
TIME 3 hours 30 minutes

Swap ins

Oxtail is a winner here, but you could
adapt this recipe and use shin, brisket or
short rib (you might have bought extra
when you made the Braised Short Rib on
page 94) and then cook in the same way.

My Auntie Wendy cooked an oxtail casserole for
me when I was about 15 years old and it stuck in
my memory like glue. Comforting and wholesome,
it embodied my favourite kind of sharing supper;
all in one pot, a stew that's rich in flavour, affordable
ingredients and shouts humble, home-cooking.
This is what British food is to me, and boy do I
love it. I remember badgering Wendy for the recipe
and like all the best recipes, she always said, 'Oh I
can't remember, bit of this and probably some of
that ...' so here is my version, hoping to do Wendy's
some justice.

Ask your butcher to chop up the oxtail. Add the oxtail
to a large bowl, season well and toss in the flour.

In the large casserole, heat a drizzle of vegetable oil
on a high heat and once hot, add the oxtail in batches,
browning as much as possible, about 10 minutes.
You might need to reduce the heat slightly once the
casserole comes up to temperature, but make sure
you brown the meat.

When all the meat has been browned, return all
the pieces back to the casserole, along with the onions,
carrots, celery and garlic, mix well to combine, about
1 minute, then deglaze the casserole by adding the red
wine (or a glug of stock if you aren't using wine) and
letting it bubble away, gently scraping the base of the
casserole with a wooden spoon.

Add the fresh and canned tomatoes and the beef
stock. Tie the thyme and oregano up together with
some string, chuck that into the casserole along with
the bay leaves and bring to the boil.

Reduce the heat to a low simmer and cook for
1 hour, then add the potatoes (whole), and continue to
gently simmer for another 2 hours, stirring occasionally.

Remove from the oven, taste to check for
seasoning, and let it sit for 10 minutes before serving.

Leftovers
Heat up (until piping hot) and serve as it is, it's almost better as a leftover, with some warm French baguette and salty butter. Alternatively, you could discard the bones and add it to a Bolognese ragu or cottage pie mix.

chilli & chocolate con carne

2 red (bell) peppers, deseeded
   and finely chopped
2 red onions, finely chopped
1 carrot, finely chopped
140 g/5 oz. chorizo
5 garlic cloves, grated
1 tablespoon smoked paprika
1 tablespoon cumin seeds
½ teaspoon cayenne pepper
1 teaspoon dried oregano
2 tablespoons tomato purée/paste
1 kg/35 oz. minced/ground beef
300 ml/1¼ cups beef stock
2 x 400-g/14-oz. cans chopped tomatoes
1 can red kidney beans
30 g/1 oz. dark chocolate (at least 70%)
3 spring onions/scallions, to serve
200 ml/scant 1 cup soured/sour
   cream, to serve

SERVES 6–8
TIME 2 hours

Swap ins
Swap smoked bacon for chorizo and
sweet paprika, ground cumin or fresh
oregano for their counterparts. Fresh
parsley or coriander/cilantro can step
in for spring onions/scallions.

Leftovers
See page 67. Or make sloppy Giuseppe-
style sandwiches with melted mozzarella.

I've added chorizo to intensify the meatiness and
some chocolate to give the chilli a subtle sweetness at
the end. This recipe is best served with Dill & Basil Rice
(see page 124) or plenty of salad and some garlic bread.

Heat a drizzle of vegetable oil in a large casserole or
saucepan and, once hot, add the chopped (bell) pepper,
frying vigorously, achieving a rich colour and moderate
char, for about 3–4 minutes.

Scoop out the charred red (bell) peppers from the
pan, transfer to a bowl and reduce the heat to medium.
Add the onions and carrot to the pan (with another
drizzle of oil if you need). Sweat for 10 minutes, until
softening and beginning to colour.

Meanwhile, halve the chorizo piece lengthways,
then finely chop. Next, add the chorizo to the cooking
onions and carrot. Fry for 3 minutes, stirring very often,
and then return the charred (bell) peppers back to
the pan, along with the garlic, paprika, cumin seeds,
cayenne pepper and oregano. Mix all the ingredients
until fragrant, 30 seconds, then add the tomato purée
and let cook out for 2 minutes.

Add the beef to the pan, break up using a wooden
spoon and fry for 5 minutes until well-browned.

Finally, add the beef stock and canned tomatoes
and bring to the boil. Once boiling, reduce the heat to
a gentle bubble and simmer for 2 hours, stirring often.
If the chilli reduces too quickly, add a splash of water
to prevent it drying out.

Whilst the chilli cooks, drain and rinse the kidney
beans, break up the chocolate, finely slice the spring
onion and season the soured/sour cream.

When the chilli has been on the hob for 90 minutes,
add the kidney beans and chocolate and stir well to
combine, then simmer for the remaining 30 minutes.
Taste to check for seasoning and simmer gently on a
low heat for a final 5 minutes.

Serve with the spring onions/scallions on top and
soured/sour cream on the side.

on the side

From salads to starches, crisps to chips; a selection of some of my favourite 'sides' that complement loads of the savoury mains, or for piling up as a mezze, roast or BBQ spread.

apple & kale salad

The sweetness of an apple and the super savouriness of kale and Parmesan are what make this salad marvellous. I made it for a picnic once, another fridge-raid bowl that turned out pretty nicely, and is now one of my go-to combinations. I've added asparagus to the recipe as it goes well, but if it's not the right time of the year, simply leave it out. You could replace it with something like French beans or just more broccoli, again, experiment with whatever is around, I'm sure it will be great.

100 g/3½ oz. Tenderstem broccoli
   (or standard broccoli)
100 g/3½ oz. asparagus (if in season)
100 g/3½ oz. kale
1 lemon
1 Braeburn apple
100 g/3½ oz. rocket/arugula
2 tablespoons extra virgin olive oil
25 g/1 oz. Parmesan, grated
sea salt and freshly ground black
   pepper
olive oil, for roasting

SERVES 4
TIME 25 minutes

Leftovers

I love this salad loaded up in a baguette with some very mature Cheddar cheese, some chutney and roasted ham or just serve it up as it is with some extra salad leaves folded through.

Preheat the oven to 200°C fan/220°C/425°F/Gas 7.

Halve the broccoli widthways, and trim the base of the asparagus. If you're using standard broccoli, then chop up, including the trunk, into small florets.

Add the broccoli and asparagus to a large baking sheet, drizzle with olive oil and season. Toss to coat and then bake on the top shelf of the oven for 8 minutes.

Add the kale to a large salad bowl and drizzle with a small amount of olive oil, season and then toss, crunching slightly with your hands to combine.

Core and quarter the apple and thinly slice each quarter lengthways. Halve the lemon and then squeeze some juice over the apple slices.

Once the vegetables have had 8 minutes, remove from the oven and tip the kale on top, then spread out. Return to the oven for another 10–12 minutes, until the kale is crispy, but not burnt.

Add the apple slices, rocket/arugula, extra virgin olive oil, grated Parmesan and a good squeeze of lemon juice to the salad bowl and set aside.

Once the greens are ready, let them cool down on the baking sheet for 5 minutes, then add to the salad bowl and toss well to combine. Season to taste and serve.

Swap ins

Swap in any greens you like. Use whatever's in season if you can. The rocket/arugula can be any salad, baby leaf salad works well with this dish too. Any firm, crunchy apple variety, such as a Cox's apple, is fine. Parmesan can be Pecorino or any hard Italian cheese. Swap the lemon for a lime, too, but you might need more than one.

raw fennel, chive & dill salad

Raw vegetables, in my opinion, far exceed cooked vegetables. I'm not sure if that's from eating overcooked vegetables at school or just the fact that my favourite texture is crunch. This super simple, five-ingredient salad is a failsafe and fresh accompaniment to meat, fish or vegetable dishes and its day (or two) old leftovers also work really well in my pasta bake recipe (see page 59). It's also one of the quickest recipes you'll make in the book.

4 fennel bulbs
20 g/¾ oz. fresh chives
10 g/⅓ oz. fresh dill
2 lemons
3 tablespoons olive oil
sea salt and freshly ground black
** pepper**

SERVES 6
TIME 10 minutes

Trim the base of the fennel bulbs (and remove the outer layer, but only if they're particularly gnarly), then thinly slice the whole vegetable widthways. Cut the chives in half widthways, tear up the dill (removing only the base of the stalks) and add them all to a large salad bowl.

Halve the lemons and squeeze the juice over the fennel and herbs, then drizzle over the olive oil and some seasoning. Toss well to combine, taste to check for seasoning and let it sit for 5 minutes before serving.

Swap ins
Mint is a wonderful addition or swap it in for either the chives or dill. Lemon juice could be lime and try other oils.

Leftovers
Go to page 59 for a pasta bake recipe, using this leftover, and quite possibly now soggy, salad.

blackened romano pepper, tomato & chilli salad

4 romano peppers
200 g/7 oz. tomatoes, finely chopped
1 green chilli/chile, deseeded and
    finely chopped
10 g/⅓ oz. freshly chopped parsley
10 g/⅓ oz. freshly chopped
    coriander/cilantro
1 tablespoon pomegranate molasses
1 teaspoon good-quality balsamic
    vinegar
1 teaspoon olive oil
sea salt and freshly ground black
    pepper

SERVES 4
TIME 25 minutes

Swap ins
You can use (bell) peppers instead
of Romano and any tomatoes are fine
here. Swap in balsamic glaze instead
of molasses and any vinegar you like,
but red wine vinegar would be my first
replacement option.

Leftovers
Serve cold with literally anything, or fold
into a pasta sauce or ragu or use as a
relish-type addition to a sandwich!

This recipe works well on the hob/stovetop, but
is particularly great if you can char the peppers on
a barbecue/outdoor grill. It takes the same amount
of time as in a frying pan/skillet, so no edits or time
needed for either method. There's some chopping to
do, but settle in and practice your knife skills, mix it
all up and serve! It's lovely sat alongside some of the
other salads, see pages 154–157 for some menu ideas.

Turn the barbecue/outdoor grill on if you're using it.
If not, heat a large, dry frying pan/skillet on a high
heat (no oil).

Pierce the Romano peppers a few times to allow
steam to escape freely during cooking.

Add the Romano peppers to the hot barbecue/
grill or frying pan/skillet and char on a high heat for
15 minutes, until well blackened, but not necessarily
tender. They don't need to be really soft, so focus on
charring, over the cooking.

Once you are happy with them, remove from the
heat and cool on the side and whilst they cool, prep
the rest of the ingredients.

Add the tomatoes, chilli/chile, herbs, molasses,
vinegar, olive oil and some seasoning to a bowl and
set aside.

Remove the stalks and seeds from the Romano
peppers then finely chop the flesh. Add it to the bowl,
then mix well to combine. Taste to check for seasoning
and then serve.

red cos & seed salad & jam jar dressing

FOR THE SALAD
3 shallots
100 g/3½ oz. mixed seeds
2 heads red cos lettuce
20 g/¾ oz. fresh mint
sea salt and freshly ground black
  pepper
olive oil, for cooking

FOR THE DRESSING
1 garlic clove
40 ml/1¼ fl oz. olive oil
40 ml/1¼ fl oz. red wine vinegar
1 heaped teaspoon Dijon mustard
1 heaped teaspoon grainy mustard
½ teaspoon English mustard
1 heaped teaspoon mango chutney
1 teaspoon maple syrup
½ teaspoon sea salt
¼ teaspoon freshly ground black
  pepper
juice of ½ lemon
1 teaspoon sesame oil
1 teaspoon pomegranate molasses

SERVES 6
TIME 40 minutes

I grew up on punchy salad dressings. I could drink the stuff (have drunk the stuff), I love it so much. This triple mustard vinaigrette has been included in homage to my late Grandma Mouse and her children, to include my father and two aunties, who are all amazing home-cooks, each with enviable skills of (but by no means limited to) whipping up a lip-smacking dressing. The salad is great too, but if I'm honest, it's a mere vessel for the star of the show.

Preheat the oven to 200°C fan/220°C/425°F/Gas 7.

Halve the shallots (skin-on) and add to a small baking sheet, drizzle with olive oil and sprinkle with a pinch of seasoning. Rub with your hands to coat in the oil and bake on the middle shelf of the preheated oven for 30 minutes, until browned, soft and caramelized.

Meanwhile, heat a large frying pan/skillet over a medium-high heat and, once hot, add the seeds. Toast for about 5 minutes, tossing often, until golden and popping. Transfer to a plate to cool.

Make the dressing by peeling and bashing the garlic clove, then add all the ingredients to a jar (preferably an almost-empty condiment jar, such as mustard or a sweet chutney), seal with the lid and shake very well. Taste to check for seasoning.

Tear the base of the red cos heads off, then separate the leaves into a large salad bowl. Next, separate the mint leaves from their stalks and add the leaves to the bowl, along with the toasted seeds. Separate the roasted shallot layers (discarding the skins) and add them too, then dress with a healthy glug of jam jar dressing and toss to combine.

Swap ins

Use any lettuce leaves you like, but a large leaf with a firm structure and good crunch is best, such as Romaine, Little Gem or iceberg. Small onions instead of shallots are fine and the dressing can be swapped in with so many variants. Try different chutneys, vinegars, sweeteners and see what you like best!

Leftovers

Keep the dressing in the fridge in the sealed jar for up to 10 days. Remove and replace the garlic, if necessary, as that is often the first thing to get a bit 'old'.

polenta croutons

These croutons are a great accompaniment to the Red Cos & Seed Salad & Jam Jar Dressing (see opposite) as a trio, or a brilliant alternative to chips, as a side or snack. They freeze well and are super crispy and crunchy. If you have any leftover caper and lemon yogurt from the Fish & Chips recipe (see page 64), get that out of the fridge and use as a dip.

250 ml/1 cup plus 1 tablespoon
   vegetable stock
75 g/2¾ oz. polenta, and extra
   for baking
50 g/1¾ oz. Parmesan, grated
¼ teaspoon dried chilli/hot red
   pepper flakes
5 g/⅛ oz. tarragon leaves, roughly
   chopped
sea salt and freshly ground black
   pepper
olive oil, for baking

SERVES 4–6
TIME 45 minutes

Preheat the oven to 210°C fan/230°C/450°F/Gas 8.

Add the vegetable stock to a medium saucepan and bring to just below a simmer. Add the polenta and stir continuously, until all the liquid has been absorbed, the polenta is thick and coming away from the pan. It'll only take a couple of minutes or so.

Next, add the Parmesan, dried chilli/hot red pepper flakes, tarragon and some seasoning. Mix very well to combine, then transfer to a plate covered with parchment paper. Leave to cool to room temperature, about 20 minutes.

If you're going to freeze some, it's best to freeze it at this stage (once cool), then when you have fully defrosted the set polenta, continue from the next step, below.

Sprinkle some extra polenta onto a baking sheet. Break up the set and cooled polenta into rough croutons (just tear up like you would when making bread croutons, the size really doesn't matter much) and add to the baking sheet. Spread them out and sprinkle a little more extra polenta on top.

Drizzle over some olive oil and put onto the top shelf of the preheated oven. Bake for 25 minutes, until really crispy.

Serve warm or cold as salad croutons (although I leave them on the side so they don't go soggy), snacks, canapés or chip/potato alternatives).

Swap ins
Most other hard cheeses would be delicious, and any other soft herb too. You need the polenta, but chicken stock could work and replacing the chilli flakes with other spices would be great too.

Leftovers
Store in the fridge for up to 48 hours and heat up (and regain some crunch) by placing in a hot oven for 15 minutes.

roasted shallots with green yogurt

My favourite way to cook all onions is just as they are. Keeping the skin on gives the shallots (and all alliums) a natural jacket, letting the layers soften and caramelize, whilst protecting the delicate flesh from burning or drying out. It also means the prep is minimal and that the edible part (all but the outer layers of brittle skin) almost gets braised in its own juices. Glorious. Serve the roasted shallots with the quickest sauce ever – all it calls for is some leftover pesto, chimichurri or salsa and natural/plain yogurt. Bob's your uncle and so on …

Swap ins
Any other type of onions, just make sure that when you cut them, keep a part of the root intact through each slice, so the layers remain attached to one another at the base. The green part of the sauce can literally be any type of herby, oily sauce – and if you don't have any, make a pesto.

Leftovers
They're great served cold and thrown into salads or sandwiches, just pull off the outer skin and discard. The green yogurt is fine in the fridge in an airtight container for up to 3 days, and lovely with meat, fish, in sarnies or as a dip for crudités... or my favourite, Baked Potato Skins and Potato Peel Crisps (pages 120–121).

6–8 shallots
60 g/2¼ oz. herb-based cold sauce such
    as pesto, salsa or chimichurri
80 g/3 oz. natural/plain yogurt
sea salt and freshly ground black pepper
olive oil, for roasting

SERVES 4–6
TIME 50 minutes

Preheat the oven to 180°C fan/200°C/400°F/Gas 6.

Halve the shallots (skin-on) lengthways and add them all to a large baking sheet. Drizzle over some olive oil and season well. Toss to coat the shallots and then place on the top shelf of the oven and roast for 40 minutes.

Mix the herb sauce and yogurt in a small bowl, with a pinch of salt and pepper (taste to check for seasoning).

When the shallots are done, let them sit for 5 minutes, then transfer to a serving dish and spoon over the green yogurt. Pass around some napkins and encourage people to enjoy with their hands, like mussels!

date, goat's cheese & cavolo nero casarecce

This recipe is a real sweet and savoury mash-up. There are plenty of salty notes from the cavolo nero, Parmesan and lardons, then the Medjool dates even the whole dish up with their sticky-sweet hit. I love this salad as a main course or side salad at a barbecue. It also lasts for a few days, so pile the leftovers on top of some crunchy salad leaves and have as a packed lunch or picnic.

200 g/7 oz. cavolo nero
240 g/8¾ oz. casarecce
  (or any dried pasta)
200 g/7 oz. smoked lardons
180 g/6¼ oz. Medjool dates
1 lemon
40 g/1½ oz. Parmesan, grated
75 g/2¾ oz. soft goat's cheese
sea salt and freshly ground black
  pepper
olive oil, for cooking
extra virgin olive oil, for dressing

SERVES 6
TIME 25 minutes

Preheat the oven to 200°C fan/220°C/425°F/Gas 7.

Slice the cavolo nero into 2–3 cm/¾–1¼ inch thick slices and place on a baking sheet, then drizzle with olive oil and seasoning. Place on the top shelf of the preheated oven and bake for 12 minutes, until cooked and crisp. Set aside.

Meanwhile, bring a large pan of salted water to the boil and, once boiling, add the pasta and cook according to the package instructions, minus 1 minute to achieve an al dente bite. Drain the pasta and rinse under cold water to stop the cooking.

In a non-stick frying pan/skillet, add a drizzle of olive oil and warm up on a high heat. Once hot, add the lardons and fry until they're golden brown, about 6 minutes. Remove from the heat and let them sit in the pan still sizzling, until they cool down.

Tear the dates in half and remove (then discard) the stones/pits, then roughly chop into smallish pieces.

Halve the lemon. Add the crispy cavolo nero, cooked pasta, dates, Parmesan, smoked lardons (avoiding pouring in the pan oil) and squeezed lemon juice to the bowl, followed by the goat's cheese, which is best to just spoon apart in big chunks and throw in. Add a generous drizzle of extra virgin olive oil. Fold through to combine (but avoid mixing vigorously, as you want the goat's cheese to remain in chunks), then serve.

Swap ins
Any pasta will do, as will standard dates. You can use bacon and chop it up once it's cooked and crispy instead of lardons, and the Parmesan is quite important but play around with other cheeses in place of goat's cheese.

Leftovers
This dish lasts well in an airtight container in the fridge for up to 3 days, so fold some salad through it and use up as packed lunches or picnics with an extra glug of extra virgin olive oil.

coriander & black onion slaw

Coleslaw can so easily, in my opinion, be too heavy on the mayonnaise and not big enough on flavour. This is a fresh and fragrant version that goes wonderfully with the Blackened Romano Pepper, Tomato & Chilli Salad (see page 108), Dill & Basil Rice (see page 124) and any meat or fish dish you want. Please don't bother peeling the carrots before you grate them. A quick rinse under cold water is fine, the skin is just as nutritious and delicious as the rest of the vegetable.

40 g/1½ oz. fresh ginger
2 limes
20 g/¾ oz. fresh mint
400 g/14 oz. carrots, coarsely grated
30 g/1 oz. freshly chopped coriander/
    cilantro
1 garlic clove, grated
1 tablespoon black onion seeds/
    nigella seeds
1 tablespoon olive oil
1 teaspoon sesame oil
sea salt and freshly ground black
    pepper

SERVES 4
TIME 10 minutes

Peel and grate the ginger (making sure you catch all of the juice). Finely zest the limes. Separate the mint leaves from their hardy stalks (discarding the stalks and leaving the leaves whole).

Add all of the prepped ingredients to a mixing bowl, with the black onion seeds, olive oil and sesame oil, then squeeze in all the juice from the limes too.

Add a pinch of salt and pepper to the bowl, then mix well to combine, and taste to check for seasoning before serving.

Leftovers
It's wonderful still for up to 2 days, kept sealed in the fridge, and use it as a side salad, folded into the Asian Chicken Salad (see page 92) or served with the Sweet Potato Baked Eggs (see page 29).

Swap ins

If you don't have nigella seeds, use black sesame seeds. Fresh coriander/cilantro and mint can be replaced with fresh parsley or basil. Fresh ginger is quite important, but use ginger paste if you have to. Limes are also important, but use 1 lemon if that's what you have. Olive oil you need, but any nut oil is fine to replace the sesame oil.

baked potato skins with butter

Make this genius snack when you have leftover potato skin halves, having made mashed potato with baked potato flesh (the best way to make particularly flavoursome mash). My friend's mother, Georgie, who is a caterer, made these years ago when we were staying at her house and I've been obsessed with them ever since. They're best in an AGA, but as most of us don't have one of those, we can make do in a normal oven! Eat them like a cracker or toast and you'll never look back.

baked potato skins, flesh removed
sea salt, to serve
butter, to serve
cheese, to serve

SERVES 2–4
TIME 20 minutes

Preheat the oven to 200°C fan/220°C/425°F/ Gas 7.

Put the empty baked potato skins on a baking sheet and bake in the oven for 15–20 minutes to crisp up very well.

Let them sit for a minute before serving, then pop them on a board with butter, sea salt and cheese. I also love them with Marmite, and think that you might too.

potato peel crisps

peel from 1 kg/35 oz. of potatoes
    (I use red potatoes)
½ teaspoon smoked paprika
sea salt and freshly ground black
    pepper
olive oil, for baking

SERVES 2–4
TIME 35 minutes

Chuck the peel on a non-stick baking sheet with a glug of olive oil, the smoked paprika and generous amounts of sea salt and black pepper.

Toss well to coat and roast on the top shelf of the oven for 30 minutes; shake and turn a couple of times during cooking.

Cool on the sheet, tossing a couple of times, and either eat immediately as a cooking snack or transfer to a sealable container… although mine seldom make it past the baking sheet…

Swap ins

You can use any potato that you have for these recipes, but what I have suggested work best for me. The smoked paprika can be swapped with literally any dried herb or spice for the crisps – experiment! The jacket potato skins get cooked as they are without any other ingredients, so serve with whatever takes your fancy – use up what you have at home and get inventive.

Leftovers

Store in an airtight container at room temperature for up to 24 hours, but they're best thrown on a baking sheet and re-crisped up briefly in a hot oven. Enjoy as they are or crumble up and use as a garnish in salads, on soups, like croutons, or a crunchy topping for the Chilli & Chocolate Con Carne (see page 101).

roasted carrots & legumes with pink peppercorns & parsley

I served this recipe as one of the side dishes at my supper club, which I held in November-time. It was a warming, earthy side dish as part of a winter menu, but I have since then also served it at summer barbecues, so it really is enjoyable at any time of the year. The crispy, popped legumes which will capture the hearts of even the least adventurous, potentially young among us. If you're cooking for children, maybe grind the pink peppercorns a little to avoid them getting a whole one mid-bite.

6 carrots (or 12 baby carrots)
400-g/14-oz. can chickpeas, drained and rinsed
400-g/14-oz. can haricot beans, drained and rinsed
8 garlic cloves (skin-on)
3 tablespoons olive oil
2 teaspoons sea salt
2 teaspoons pink peppercorns
10 g/⅓ oz. fresh parsley

SERVES 4–6
TIME 65 minutes

Preheat the oven to 200°C fan/220°C/425°F/Gas 7.

Halve the carrots lengthways (if you're using baby, or just slim carrots, leave whole). Add the prepped carrots, chickpeas, haricot beans, garlic cloves, olive oil, salt and peppercorns to a large baking sheet and toss well to coat. Roast on the top shelf of the preheated oven for 1 hour, turning halfway through cooking.

Once ready, remove from the oven, roughly chop the parsley and then fold through the roasted carrots and legumes. Serve immediately.

Swap ins
Swap potatoes (standard and sweet), celeriac and parsnips for carrots. Chickpeas and haricot beans can be swapped for other legumes such as cannellini beans, but avoid butter/lima beans as they tend to dry out and go chalky.

Leftovers
This recipe reheats well, so add it back to a baking sheet and roast for 15–20 minutes, until it is piping hot. That, or blitz into a hearty soup with more cooked root vegetables and vegetable stock, with a dollop of soured/sour cream at the end.

dill & basil rice

This recipe is an ode to, and in admiration of, the women at the Hubb Community Kitchen, London. I was lucky enough to work on the cookbook 'Together' as a co-recipe tester and food stylist with my friend Val Berry, the team at Ebury Press and HRH The Duchess of Sussex. The recipe below is inspired by Ahlam Saeid's 'Green Rice', which I insist you cook immediately (if you haven't already). My much inferior version is a speedy, veggie side dish that I've adapted and developed, inspired by Ahlam's genius. A modern moment of nostalgia, reminding me of a project I was honoured to work on ... whilst using up limping herbs and storecupboard staples of course!

400 g/14 oz. basmati rice
20 g/¾ oz. fresh dill
10 g/⅓ oz. fresh basil
1 lemon
2 tablespoons dried dill
1 tablespoon olive oil
sea salt and freshly ground black
   pepper

SERVES 4–6
TIME 15 minutes

Cook the rice according to package instructions.

Whilst the rice cooks, remove any hardy stalks from the dill and roughly chop. Next, remove the basil leaves from the stalks. Finely slice the stalks and keep the leaves whole. Halve the lemon.

When the rice is cooked and drained, add it to a serving bowl, along with the prepped fresh herbs, dried dill, olive oil and some seasoning. Add a squeeze of lemon juice, fold the ingredients together to combine and taste to check for seasoning.

Serve immediately.

Swap ins
The most important combination for this dish is the dried and fresh dill, but I would happily add any soft herbs I have lying around. Coriander/cilantro, parsley, a little tarragon too.

Leftovers
Serve cold as leftovers or you could try reheating (until piping hot) and whipping up a herby stir-fry or egg-fried rice.

proper oven chips

Chips are my favourite side dish. It's not a glamorous or refined choice, but I don't care. They're just perfect. Here's an unremarkable but utterly failsafe recipe to make great chips, every time, without the faff of deep-frying. You'll need a large, non-stick baking sheet, but other than that, nothing special at all... just an appetite and ketchup or mayo, whichever way you sway.

Swap ins
Use other potatoes if you need to but the minimal ingredients above are the best for the job. Rapeseed oil is essentially vegetable oil (oil that is labelled vegetable oil is very often rapeseed oil in the UK, which is the best out of the cheap, high-burning-point oils, in my opinion), but you can also use sunflower oil.

Leftovers
Reheat in a hot oven for 5 minutes until piping hot and enjoy as they are, or you could make loaded chips (like nachos) and place on a baking sheet, topped with grated cheese and chilli/chile slices, remove and finish with spring onions/scallions and soured/sour cream (add some leftover chilli con carne from page 101 under the cheese too, if you have some!)

1 kg/35 oz. Maris Piper or King Edward potatoes
5 tablespoons vegetable oil
sea salt

SERVES 4–6
TIME 1 hour

Preheat the oven to 200°C fan/220°C/425°F/Gas 7.

Fill a large saucepan with well-salted water and bring to the boil.

Rinse the potatoes, then cut into thick chips/wedges. Add the potatoes (raw) to your largest non-stick baking sheet and if they can all fit on a single layer then great, if not, then you'll need a second baking sheet, so grab one now.

Once the water is boiling, add the raw cut chips/wedges to the saucepan, bring back to the boil and once boiling, bubble for 5–6 minutes, until par-cooked.

When you're about to drain the potatoes, add the vegetable oil to your baking sheet(s) and heat up in the preheated oven.

Drain the chips/wedges then set them back in the colander, sit the colander on top of the saucepan (off the heat) and let them steam for 3 minutes.

Jiggle the chips/wedges around in the colander to create some fluffy/scruffy edges.

Carefully remove the hot oil sheet(s) from the oven and, standing back to avoid any spluttering hot oil, pour the steamed, fluffed chips/wedges onto the baking sheet(s). Season then shake to spread out.

Transfer to the oven and bake for 15 minutes. Remove the sheet(s) from the oven then shake and turn the chips/wedges. Bake for another 15 minutes, shake and turn again and return to the oven for a final 5 minutes. Once they are ready, shake once more, season with an extra pinch of sea salt (important to do this whilst they're really hot) and serve immediately.

sweet things

As 'not really a pudding person', but more of a 'something sweet' opportunist, here's a sweet batch of honestly simple snacks, puddings, presents and treats (sweet-tooth or not).

ginger & sesame marshmallows

I'd never been that fussed about marshmallows until I made proper home-made ones for the first time when recipe testing years ago. They were a delicious raspberry ripple recipe and I couldn't believe how light and luxurious they were. They are great as homemade gifts, petits fours, or just good to have around when you're in need of a sweet treat.

7 gelatine leaves
15 ml/1 tablespoon liquid glucose
250 g/1¼ cups golden caster/
   superfine sugar
100 ml/⅓ cup plus 1 tablespoon
   water
1 lemon wedge
3 egg whites
4 tablespoons cornflour/cornstarch
2 tablespoons sesame seeds
100 g/3½ oz. stem ginger,
   drained and finely chopped
¼ teaspoon sea salt
1½ tablespoons stem ginger syrup
1 tablespoon icing/confectioners'
   sugar

a sugar thermometer
20.5-cm/8-inch non-stick brownie
   pan, greased

MAKES 16
TIME 35 minutes,
   plus overnight setting

Add the gelatine leaves to a bowl of cold water to soften.

Put the liquid glucose, sugar and water into a small saucepan and let dissolve over a low heat. Once dissolved, increase the heat to medium-high and let it bubble away until the liquid reaches 125°C/257°F.

Wipe the inside of a stand mixer bowl and whisk attachment with the lemon wedge to remove any traces of grease, then add the egg whites. Whisk on a medium setting to start, then increase to high until stiff peaks form. Continue whisking on high and gradually pour in the hot sugar syrup, taking care to avoid too much splatter on the side of the bowl. Next, add the soft gelatine leaves (squeezing out any excess water with your hands before you add to the bowl) and let the marshmallow mixture whisk for a further 10 minutes, until the bowl feels cool on the outside and the marshmallow looks glossy.

Tip 3 tablespoons of the cornflour/starch into the greased brownie pan. Shake the pan around to coat the surface with the cornflour/starch, then tap the pan on the work surface to let the excess settle on the base.

Toast the seseme seeds in a small frying pan/skillet over a medium heat for 2–3 minutes. Once golden, transfer to a small bowl to cool.

Once the marshmallow has had 10 minutes, add the sea salt, stem ginger and syrup to the bowl and whisk on a low speed for a further 30 seconds.

Transfer the marshmallow mixture to the prepared brownie pan and sprinkle the sesame seeds over the top. Leave to set overnight (or for at least 4 hours) in a cool, dry place, but not in the fridge.

Once the marshmallow is set, mix the remaining cornflour/starch and the sugar together and sprinkle onto a clean surface. Slice into 16 pieces and gently toss in the cornflour/sugar mix to lightly coat the sides. Seal in an airtight container and consume within 3 days.

Swap ins
You need all of the ingredients from
the list but you could use a combination
of white and black sesame seeds if you
have them. White caster/superfine sugar
is also fine.

Leftovers
Chop up the marshmallows and
add them to a rocky road!

baked rosemary & nutmeg nectarines

5 sprigs fresh rosemary
4 ripe nectarines, halved and
    stoned/pitted
¼ whole nutmeg
2 tablespoons soft light brown sugar
a pinch of sea salt
1 tablespoon olive oil
Greek yogurt, to serve

SERVES 4
TIME 30 minutes

Swap ins

Use peaches or plums instead
of nectarines. Try thyme instead
of rosemary and ground
cinnamon instead
of nutmeg.

Rosemary and fruit is a joy. Nutmeg is such a
warming spice, one that I think works wonderfully
with the summery sweet tang of a nectarine,
mellowed by baking in the oven. These are a great
quick desserts for guests, or brilliant for weekend
breakfasts too.

Preheat the oven to 180°C fan/200°C/400°F/Gas 6.
    Lay the rosemary sprigs on a small baking dish,
and top with the nectarines, cut-side up.
    Finely grate a dash of nutmeg over each halve, then
sprinkle the sugar on top, followed by a small pinch of
sea salt. Drizzle over the olive oil and transfer to the
top shelf of the preheated oven. Let bake for 25–30
minutes, until lightly coloured and very soft.
    Serve with Greek yogurt, porridge or rice pudding.
Store any leftovers in an airtight container in the
fridge for up to 3 days.

Leftovers
Lovely served with my rice
pudding (see page 135) or
chilled and served on a cheese
board instead of quince jelly.

Swap ins

Risotto rice can be used instead of
pudding rice, you can use semi-skimmed
milk, and replace the cream with milk if
you don't have any. Vanilla paste is fine,
use 1 teaspoon and add with the milk.

rice pudding and balsamic strawberries

A rice pudding doesn't have to be extraordinary to be comforting and delicious. As long as the rice is cooked fully, there's plenty of creaminess and some sort of jam/jelly to go with it, I'm happy. The balsamic strawberries are a nice and quick compote option instead of jam/jelly. You can do this on the hob instead of the oven, it'll take about 45 minutes to an hour, and make sure you've got some spare milk or water to add splashes along the way, should it dry out.

FOR THE RICE PUDDING
110 g/4 oz. pudding rice
170 ml/¾ cup single/light cream
620 ml/scant 2¾ cups full fat milk
3 tablespoons golden caster sugar
¼ teaspoon mixed spice
a good pinch of sea salt
1 vanilla pod

FOR THE BALSAMIC STRAWBERRIES
200 g/2 cups strawberries
3 tablespoons caster sugar
2 tablespoons balsamic vinegar

a 1.5 litre/6 cups plus 4 tablespoons baking dish, greased with butter

SERVES 4–6
TIME 2 hour 5 minutes

Leftovers
Reheat in a pan with a good splash of milk, and make sure it's piping hot before you serve.

Preheat the oven to 140°C fan/160°C/325°F/Gas 3.

Add the pudding rice, cream, milk, sugar, mixed spice and salt to the prepared baking dish.

Halve the vanilla pod/bean lengthways, then scrape out the seeds. Add the seeds and pod/bean halves to the baking dish too. Mix well to combine (whilst trying to avoid scraping off the butter from the dish), transfer to the middle shelf of the preheated oven and let bake for 2 hours (stirring halfway through) until the rice is fully cooked and there is a golden skin on top.

Meanwhile, remove the stalks from the strawberries and halve them. Add the strawberries to a saucepan with the sugar, balsamic vinegar and 2 tablespoons water. Bring to the boil and then bubble away for about 5 minutes, until the strawberries have broken down and the liquid turns syrupy, making sure you stir often. Remove from the heat and cool.

Remove the rice pudding from the oven, stand for a couple of minutes and then serve with the balsamic strawberry compote.

fruit & nut tart

This is a great recipe for clearing out the cupboard. Old chocolate, dried fruit, nuts, flour, sugar, the lot. Make the pastry in advance, if you like. It's a dessert served cold, so it's great for a dinner party without any 'à la minute' cooking necessary.

FOR THE PASTRY
100 g/½ cup minus 1 tablespoon
    butter, cubed
1 egg
1 egg yolk
200 g/1½ cups plain/all-purpose
    flour, plus extra for dusting
80 g/⅔ cup sifted icing/
    confectioners' sugar
¼ teaspoon sea salt

FOR THE GANACHE
80 g/3 oz. dried fruit (I use raisins,
    sultanas and cranberries, plus
    extra to decorate
80 g/3 oz. chopped nuts (such as
    hazelnuts, almonds, walnuts,
    pistachios), plus extra to decorate
200 ml/scant 1 cup double/heavy cream
200 g/7 oz. dark/bittersweet or
    milk chocolate (or a mixture),
    broken into small chunks
30 ml/2 tablespoons whole milk

*a 23-cm/9-inch diameter tart case
parchment paper and baking beans
    or dry rice*

SERVES 8–10
TIME 1 hour, plus chilling

Swap ins

You can use flavoured chocolates
if you like too, chocolates with a hint
of orange or mint are great.

Put the cubed butter in the freezer for 5 minutes.

Add the egg and egg yolk to a mug and whisk with a fork. Next, add the flour, sugar and salt to a food processor and pulse to combine. Add the chilled butter to the flour mixture and blitz for 30 seconds, until it resembles breadcrumbs. Pour in half of the egg mixture and blitz again to bring the dough together, adding a bit more egg if needed. Work the dough for as little time as possible. As soon as it resembles pastry dough, tip onto a work surface, bring together with your hands, very briefly, wrap in a large reusable freezer bag and chill for at least an hour, or preferably overnight.

Remove the pastry from the fridge 30 minutes before you roll out. Roll the pastry out onto a well-floured surface, 3–5 mm/⅛–¼ inch thickness, roll up loosely onto the rolling pin and put on top of the tart case. Rip an overhanging corner of pastry off, roll it into a ball and dip it in flour. Nudge the pastry into the rivets of the case, using the ball. Place the lined tart case on a baking sheet, put back in the large freezer bag, seal and place in the fridge for at least 40 minutes.

Preheat the oven to 180°C fan/200°C/400°F/Gas 6.

Tear off a large piece of parchment paper and scrunch it up, then stretch out again. Retrieve the chilled pastry from the fridge and place the parchment paper on top. Pour the baking beans onto the paper, to completely fill the pastry case and place in the oven. Bake for 20 minutes, until the pastry looks sandy, dry, but still pale. Carefully remove the paper and beans or rice and return to the oven for a further 10 minutes. The pastry is done when it is dry, golden and sandy. Remove from the oven and cool on a wire rack.

Using a bread knife, carefully trim the pastry edge.

For the ganache, add the dried fruit and chopped nuts to a small bowl and set aside. Heat the cream in a medium saucepan until it's almost simmering. Remove from the heat and add the chocolate. Stir very well to melt and combine, and then fold in the milk, fruit and nuts. Pour the ganache into the tart case, then sprinkle the extra fruit and nuts around where the ganache meets the pastry edge. Chill in the fridge for at least 1½ hours (or overnight) before serving.

orange, hazelnut & caraway pavlova

This recipe has been my 'feed the hoards' go-to pudding for a while now. Pavlovas are my favourite dessert, so admittedly it's an easy win, but also because I'm obsessed with orange, hazelnut and caraway together. I developed this one for my supper club and haven't looked back. The assembly of crumbly-yet chewy meringue and nutty, spiced brittle with fresh orange, is a celebration for all. You can make the meringue a day in advance, and the brittle a week in advance, just make sure you store them both in airtight containers at room temperature.

Swap ins
This recipe is best made as is, but you could swap in the fresh oranges for blood oranges, pink/red grapefruit, nectarines or peaches, and use most nuts in place of the hazelnuts. Caraway seeds could be swapped for fennel seeds, if necessary.

Leftovers
The brittle will last for up to a week in an airtight container, stored at room temperature, however, the finished dessert will last only 1 day (stored in the fridge, and it won't look as pretty) so either finish it up as it is, or break it up and serve in individual bowls with some fresh fruit, like a golden Eton Mess!

FOR THE MERINGUE
1 lemon, cut into wedges
6 large egg whites
300 g/1½ cups golden caster/superfine sugar
1 tablespoon cornflour/cornstarch
1 teaspoon orange essence

FOR THE BRITTLE
3 teaspoons caraway seeds
300 g/1½ cups caster/granulated sugar
¼ teaspoon sea salt
80 g/⅔ cup chopped roasted hazelnuts

WHIPPED CREAM
600 ml/2½ cups double/heavy cream
1 teaspoon vanilla extract
50 g/heaping ⅓ cup icing/confectioners' sugar
2 oranges

DECORATION
2 oranges (use above, so only 2 in total needed), segmented and membrane squeezed
20 g/2 tablespoons chopped roasted hazelnuts

2 large baking sheets, lined with parchment paper

SERVES 12
TOTAL TIME 2 hours, plus cooling

Preheat the oven to 130°C fan/150°C/300°F/Gas 2.

Wipe the whisk and bowl of your stand mixer with a lemon wedge to clean it then add the egg whites to the bowl. Starting slowly, then increasing the speed, whisk until the whites reach soft peaks. Next, gradually add the sugar as the whites continue to whisk, one heaped spoonful at a time.

Once all the sugar has been incorporated, give it another 5 minutes of whisking, then rub a little meringue between your fingers. If it feels smooth, looks shiny and you can't feel any grains of sugar, it's ready. If you can, whisk it for a couple of minutes more, until smooth.

Sprinkle over the cornflour/cornstarch, orange essence and 1½ teaspoons of lemon juice (from a wedge), then whisk for another 30 seconds on medium speed to mix through. Pile the meringue onto a prepared baking sheet in a large pile, then roughly spread out to a 25 cm/9¾ inch diameter disc. Place on the middle shelf of the oven and bake for 1¾ hours. Turn off the oven and leave the meringue inside overnight to cool fully, with a wooden spoon wedged in the oven door.

Whilst the meringue bakes, make the brittle. Heat a large, non-stick frying pan/skillet over a medium heat and add the caraway seeds to toast for 2–3 minutes. Transfer to a small bowl and then wipe out the pan. Return the pan to the heat, reduce the heat to low-medium and add enough of the sugar to just cover the base of the pan. When it starts to turn to liquid, add some more sugar and continue this process until all the sugar is in the pan and has turned to liquid caramel. You can shake the pan occasionally, but do not stir with a utensil!

Once the sugar has melted to a liquid caramel, add the salt, hazelnuts and caraway seeds, very briefly fold (a heat-resistant silicone spatula is best), then quickly pour onto the second lined baking sheet. Let the mix cool completely and harden to a brittle, then break up into shards and store in an airtight container until needed.

Add the double/heavy cream, vanilla extract and icing/confectioners' sugar to a bowl, then zest the oranges over the bowl too. Whip up the cream mix with an electric or hand whisk, until stiff peaks form and then store in the fridge until needed.

Segment the zested oranges by slicing the top and bottom of each orange so it sits on a flat base, then using a small serrated knife, carve down the edge and around the curve of the orange, cutting away the skin and pith. You're essentially peeling the orange. Once 'peeled', hold the orange in your cupped hand and very carefully cut out each segment by slicing either side of each pith strip, to release a triangle/segment of orange flesh. Place the segments in a bowl and then squeeze the remaining orange membranes, over the segments to catch the juice.

Once the meringue is cool, transfer to a serving plate. Don't worry if the meringue has cracked, you're about to cover it in cream! Top with the whipped cream then decorate generously with the brittle shards, fresh orange segments, chopped hazelnuts and a little jug/pitcher of fresh orange juice on the side, to serve.

proper raspberry jelly

My Grandma Mouse used to make us grandchildren, of which there are nine, raspberry jelly/jello for dessert throughout the summer months, with raspberries from the garden. Jelly/jello and ice cream is a joyful sweet treat, whatever your age – make it in advance and serve with good-quality vanilla ice cream. I'd suggest making this when you can get in-season raspberries, too. Grandma never used to bother half-setting the jelly/jello in order to get raspberries through the entirety of the jelly/jello (I'm sure she had far more pressing things to be doing with the nine of us), so I haven't bothered either, and neither should you. Here's to all the Grandmas.

Swap ins
Strawberries are lovely for this recipe, or a mix of fresh berries would be great too. Use any cordial you have, lemon and ginger is lovely, lemongrass is a tangy and fragrant option too. You can omit the cordial altogether if you don't have any.

Leftovers
Return to the fridge to store and then consume (with more ice cream) within 2 days.

½ teaspoon vegetable oil
500 g/1 lb. 2 oz. fresh raspberries
6 gelatine leaves
200 g/1 cup caster/superfine sugar
2 tablespoons elderflower cordial
vanilla ice cream, to serve

a 600-ml/2½-cup jelly/jello mould, or 6–8 small glasses

SERVES 6–8
TIME 25 minutes, plus setting overnight

Lightly but fully grease the jelly/jello mould or glasses with the oil. Put 300 g/10½ oz. of the fresh raspberries in the mould or glasses.

Add the gelatine leaves to a small bowl with cold water and leave to soak.

Add the sugar, 450 ml/15 fl oz. water, the cordial and the remaining raspberries to a saucepan and put over a medium heat. Gently bring to just under the boil, which should take about 10 minutes. Using a potato masher or fork, gently mash the raspberries in the pan as the sugar mixture heats up. Stir often and then remove from the heat.

Pour the hot mixture through a sieve/strainer and into a measuring jug/cup, smushing the raspberry seeds in the sieve/strainer over the jug/cup, to make sure you get all the liquid through. Let it sit for 10 minutes to cool down (never add gelatine to boiling hot liquid).

Retrieve the now soft gelatine leaves from the water, squeeze out each one and add to the measuring jug/cup. Stir well to fully dissolve the gelatine and pour into your prepared mould or glasses, over the fresh raspberries. Let the jelly/jello come down to room temperature, then cover, place in the fridge and leave to set overnight.

pot luck tarte tatin

The pot luck part of the title refers to whatever (pretty much) is lurking in your fruit bowl. It's a basic tarte tatin recipe, using up whatever fruit you have, lovingly drenched in caramel and pastry – marvellous.

50 g/3½ tablespoons salted butter
100 g/½ cup caster/granulated sugar
enough fruit to cover the base of the
**   frying pan/skillet (I use 1 banana,**
**   half an apple, a nectarine and**
**   a tangerine [or half an orange])**
½ teaspoon vanilla paste
1 roll of pre-rolled puff pastry
ice cream or double/heavy cream,
**   to serve**

20-cm/8-inch diameter ovenproof
*   frying pan/skillet*

SERVES 4
TIME 55 minutes

Swap ins
You can use plum, pear, orange (no skin), tangerine (no skin), nectarine, peach, grapes, cherries (stoned/pitted), mango (no skin), banana (no skin), pineapple (no skin) – whatever you have.

Leftovers
Store in the fridge for up to 1 day. Use the leftover pastry for some Chilli Con Carne Parcels (see page 67) or see page 10 for more pastry ideas.

Preheat the oven to 160°C fan/180°C/350°F/Gas 4.

Chop up the butter into chunks and place in the fridge.

Put the oven-proof frying pan/skillet over a medium heat and sprinkle a quarter of the sugar over the base. Let the sugar dissolve and, once liquid, add another quarter of the sugar and let it dissolve. Gently shake the pan if you need to but do not stir with any sort of utensil! Continue adding the sugar as it dissolves and turns a deep, golden amber colour, about 10 minutes.

Keep an eye on the sugar, and meanwhile, prep the fruit. Halve and stone/pit any stone fruit. Peel and slice a banana into thick chunks. Cut and core an apple into wedges. Peel and thickly chop up a tangerine (or orange).

Once the sugar has dissolved, let it come to a gentle bubble and then remove from the heat immediately. Add the chilled butter and vanilla paste, then shake the pan well to melt the butter and combine. Add the fruit, cut-side-down, on top of the caramel mix, nestling it all in so it is snug and tightly fitted, in a single layer. Press it down gently to settle in the caramel too.

Next, unroll the pre-rolled pastry on top of the frying pan/skillet and, working quickly, loosely cut around the edge. Using the end of a spoon or fingers (watching you don't touch the hot caramel), fold under the pastry edge, tucking it in down the side of the frying pan/skillet. Then, using a small knife, prick a few holes over the pastry so steam can escape easily.

Bake on the top shelf of the preheated oven for 40 minutes, until the pastry is golden and the caramel is bubbling around the edge.

Remove from the oven and let it sit for 15 minutes, before inverting onto a serving plate and serving with ice cream or double/heavy cream.

rhubarb & apple crumble

We weren't much of a dessert household growing up (more of a 'have an apple if you're still hungry' vibe), however, when we did have pudding at the weekend, my Ma would often do a crumble, which we all adored. She would use cornflakes in the crumble mix to bulk out the topping, so this is a similar version using up almost-empty packets of nuts and cereals within the crumble mix. It gives extra flavour and a satisfying crunch.

10 g/2 teaspoons butter, at room temperature
400 g/14 oz. rhubarb, trimmed and cut into 4-cm/1½-inch chunks
3 medium Bramley apples, peeled, cored and cut into 4-cm/1½-inch chunks
30 g/1 oz. golden caster/granulated sugar

FOR THE TOPPING
80 g/3 oz. mixed nuts (any type)
100 g/1 stick minus 1 tablespoon butter, chilled
160 g/scant 1¼ cups plain/all-purpose flour
100 g/½ cup golden caster/granulated sugar
50 g/2 oz. granola, muesli or cornflakes
ice cream or double/heavy cream, to serve

2-litre/quart baking dish

SERVES 6–8
TIME 50 minutes

Preheat the oven to 180°C fan/200°C/400°F/Gas 6.

Rub the butter over the inside of the baking dish. Transfer the fruit to the prepped baking dish and sprinkle over the sugar, set aside.

To make the topping, roughly chop the mixed nuts and chop up the chilled butter into small chunks.

Add the flour and sugar to a large mixing bowl and briefly run your fingers through to combine. Next, add the chilled, chopped butter to the bowl. Rub the flour/sugar mix and butter together, using your fingertips and lifting your hands as you go, until it starts to resemble breadcrumbs. Finally, add in the nuts and any granola, muesli or cornflakes you have. If you're using cornflakes, crunch them up a little in your hands first. Fold through to combine, then pile the crumble on top of the fruit in the baking dish. Spread it out with your hands to cover all the fruit, then gently press down.

Transfer the crumble to the preheated oven and bake on the top shelf for 40 minutes, until the fruit is bubbling and the crumble topping is golden brown.

Let it sit for 5 minutes and then serve with ice cream or double/heavy cream…or both.

Swap ins

Most berries, pears or nectarines instead of the apples and rhubarb are good. Use wholemeal/whole-wheat flour instead of plain and a mix of caster sugar and demerara/turbinado sugar is fine too.

Leftovers

Go to page 149 for a nifty flapjack recipe using the leftover crumble in the mix.

old crumble flapjacks

Crumble is amazing as we all know, but one can never be quite sure if it's going to be all gobbled up, or if half a dish of the stuff will be left looking lonely on the side, uneaten. Make these fruity flapjacks and put any remaining crumble to good use.

300 g/10½ oz. leftover Rhubarb
    & Apple Crumble (see page 147)
280 g/10 oz. oats
120 g/1 stick plus 1 teaspoon salted
    butter
120 g/4¼ oz. syrup or honey
    (I use 50 g/maple syrup and
    70 g/2½ oz. runny honey)
100 g/½ cup soft light brown sugar
vegetable oil, for greasing

*20.5-cm/8-inch, loose-based square
    brownie pan, greased and lined with
    parchment paper*

MAKES 12
TIME 50 minutes

Swap ins
This is a leftover recipe hence the old crumble, but unsalted butter is fine, and any sugar you have will do too.

Leftovers
These really need to be consumed within 2 days, because of the fresh and roasted fruit from the crumble. They're great broken up and eaten on top of breakfast yogurt or porridge, so try that too.

Preheat the oven to 150°C fan/170°C/325°F/Gas 3.

Put the leftover rhubarb and apple crumble and the oats into a large mixing bowl and set aside.

Add the butter to a small saucepan and fully melt, then add the liquid sugars and soft light brown sugar. Continue to cook on a low heat, but only until the sugar has dissolved. Add to the large mixing bowl and mix well to combine all the ingredients.

Add the flapjack mixture to your prepped brownie pan, gently push down with the back of a spoon to even out and then bake on the top shelf of the preheated oven for 40 minutes, when the flapjack will be cooked and golden on top. Remove from the oven and allow to cool in the brownie pan. Cut into squares and serve.

peanut butter banana bread

I often make banana bread to use up not only blackening bananas, but also nuts, chocolate and sugars, that might be lying around. I rarely make one with exactly the same ingredients and, to me, that's the beauty of it. Here's one that I've created and love. I like using the crunchy kind of peanut butter for a little extra texture, but if you only have smooth, use that.

50 g/3½ tablespoons butter
330–350 g/11½–12 oz. blackened
   bananas (peeled weight),
   plus 1 spare for decoration
120 g/4½ oz. crunchy peanut butter
220 g/1⅔ cups plain/all-purpose flour
80 g/scant ½ cup caster sugar
100 g/½ cup soft light brown/
   granulated sugar
3 teaspoons baking powder
½ teaspoon sea salt
2 eggs
30 g/1 oz. salted peanuts

*900-g/2-lb. loaf pan, greased and
   lined with parchment paper*

SERVES 6–8
TIME 1¼ hours, plus cooling

Preheat the oven to 180°C fan/200°C/400°F/Gas 6.

Melt the butter in a small pan over a medium heat (or in a microwave), then remove from the heat.

Add the bananas to a bowl and mash well to break down. Add the peanut butter and melted butter to the banana bowl and mix well to combine.

In a separate, large bowl, add the flour, sugars, baking powder and sea salt. I usually don't bother with sifting, but it's worth doing so here to help with potential clumps in the brown sugar.

Mix to combine, then make a loose well in the centre. Add the eggs, loosely whisk then pile the banana mix on top and gradually combine all the ingredients together in a whisking motion, starting with the wet mix in the well.

Once all the ingredients are combined, transfer the batter to the prepped loaf pan.

Slice the remaining banana (in any way you like) and add to the top of the batter, along with the salted peanuts.

Bake in the preheated oven for 45 minutes–1 hour, until risen and baked through. Use a clean knife or skewer and poke it through the centre. If it comes out clean, the bread is cooked. If not, bake for a bit longer in 5-minute stints until done.

Transfer the loaf pan to a cooling rack, let it sit for 15 minutes in the pan, then turn out and cool fully before slicing away.

Swap ins
You can use other nut butters and sugars, just know that the loaf will be richer in flavour if you use darker sugar which might overpower the banana and peanut flavours. Add whole or chopped nuts, such as pecans or walnuts to the mix and feel free to add chocolate chunks too.

Leftovers
Staling banana bread is great for chunking up and gently frying in butter, to serve as sweet croutons with ice cream. Naughty.

welsh cakes

I might only be a quarter Welsh, but my family and I are 100% proud of our Welsh heritage, as my friends well know. Nothing reminds me more of the Gower Peninsula than a pile of freshly baked Welsh cakes. They're hugely nostalgic to me, so these have been added to the book for my family, in particular Grandad Howell, who is an unofficial Welsh cake expert.

70 g/⅓ cup minus 1 teaspoon chilled unsalted butter
1 egg
150 g/1 cup plus 2 tablespoons self-raising/rising flour, plus extra for dusting
¼ teaspoon grated nutmeg
a pinch of sea salt
40 g/1½ oz. currants or sultanas/ golden raisins
55 g/¼ cup caster/granulated sugar
vegetable oil, for frying

MAKES 8
TIME 30 minutes

Chop up the butter and place back in the fridge until needed. Add the egg to a mug and beat with a fork until combined.

Sift the flour into a mixing bowl, then add the nutmeg and salt. Mix with a metal spoon to combine.

Add the chilled butter to the mixing bowl and rub into the flour mix using your fingertips and lifting up the mix as you go. Once the mix resembles rough breadcrumbs, add the currants or sultanas/golden raisins and sugar and fold through the flour mix. Next, add the egg to the bowl and use the spoon to bring the dough together, then tip out onto a clean, lightly floured work surface and briefly knead.

Using a rolling pin (or wine bottle if you don't have one), roll out the dough to about 1 cm/⅜ inch thick, then cut into discs (using a cookie cutter, glass or mug) about 6 cm/2½ inches diameter. Once you have cut out all that you can, scrunch up the remaining dough, and roll out again to use it all up.

If you have a flat, heavy-based griddle pan, great, if not just use a frying pan/skillet for cooking the Welsh cakes. Heat up the pan to medium heat, with a small drizzle of oil, and tip the pan around in a circular motion to lightly grease the whole surface.

Add the Welsh cakes (in batches, if necessary) to the pan and cook for 2–5 minutes on each side, depending on your heat source. Cook them gently, and until golden and cooked through. Serve warm with butter and jam.

Swap ins
Cook them as they are, it's worth it.

Leftovers
Store in an airtight container for up to 2 days, then enjoy as they are or heat up in the oven, or toast and serve with butter. That, or crumble up, bake with a drizzle of oil and once golden and crispy, serve as a topping for ice cream or yogurt and fruit.

MENU PLANNER

Here are some menu plans that might come in handy, referring to a few different hosting scenarios. Read through the recipes and see what you can prep ahead to save on time. That's often what I base my menus on, as opposed to solely what I want to cook. Make sure you give yourself the chance to actually hang out with the people you're feeding!

As a general rule, if something should be crunchy/crispy it needs to be prepared for when you want to serve it, but often you can prep (whether that's chopping, roasting, etc) up until it's almost ready, then finish just before serving (that might be dressing a salad, doing the last 20 minutes roasting veg to crisp up, etc).

Secondly, always chop (if you're doing so, but most of mine go in whole or simply torn) and add fresh herbs just before serving, for any dish. If you want to get ahead, wrap them loosely in a cold, damp cloth and store in the fridge ready for when you are.

Also, you're not on washing up duty…

summer barbecue spread

Meat/fish/veg on the barbecue/outdoor grill

Coriander & black onion slaw (*page 118*)

Blackened romano pepper, tomato & chilli salad (*page 108*)

Date, goat's cheese & cavolo nero casarecce (*page 117*)

Honey, miso & soy aubergine with yogurt & coriander (*page 71*)

Soda bread boulders (*page 32*)

Proper raspberry jelly (*page 142*)

Baked rosemary & nutmeg nectarines (*page 132*)

quiet day 'à deux'

Bay-roasted grapes with black pepper
ricotta on toast (*page 22*)

Garlic & herb pasta (*page 55*)

Welsh cakes (*page 153*)

Sweet potato baked eggs (*page 29*)

Steamed greens

Tea & dark/bittersweet chocolate

winter feast

Pork chops with baked chillies & pears (*page 86*)

Apple & kale salad (*page 104*)

Roasted shallots with green yogurt
(*page 114*)

Proper oven chips (*page 127*)

Rice pudding with balsamic strawberries
(*page 135*)

full house weekend

friday night
Chilli & chocolate con carne (*page 101*)

Dill & basil rice (*page 124*)

Raw fennel, chive & dill salad (*page 107*)

Ginger & sesame marshmallows (*page 130*)

saturday
Breakfast for an army (*page 26*)

Carrot, coriander & caraway soup (*page 48*)

Chilli con carne parcels (*page 67*)

Apple & kale salad (*page 104*)

Peanut butter banana bread (*page 150*)

Lemon roasted fennel & dill pasta bake
(*page 58*)

Red cos & seed salad and
jam jar dressing (*page 110*)

Rhubarb & apple crumble
(*page 146*)

sunday
Indian scrambled eggs with naan
or toast (*page 36*)

Juices (*page 42*)

Braised chicken thighs with citrus
& greens (*page 85*)

Baked potatoes

Soda bread boulders (*page 32*)

Fruit & nut tart (*page 136*)

Old crumble flapjacks (journey snacks
for those leaving after lunch) (*page 149*)

home bird original evening meal

Potato peel crisps (*page 121*)

Braised short rib (*page 94*)

Roasted mixed squash with almonds and tarragon (*page 78*)

Roasted carrots & legumes with pink peppercorns & parsley (*page 123*)

Red cos & seed salad & jam jar dressing with Polenta croutons (*pages 110 & 111*)

Raw fennel, chive & dill salad (*page 107*)

Orange, hazelnut & caraway pavlova (*page 138*)

Spiced mint tea (*page 45*)

index

thank yous

Writing my first cookbook and being given the freedom to honestly celebrate the way I learnt to cook, the manner in which I like to feed people, and the way I endeavour to continue and expand my focus on stretching food at home, has been humbling and an utter joy. None of this would have been possible without a lot of people supporting and believing in me.

First, to Alice Sambrook, who gave Home Bird the chance to come to life. Alice came to my little supper club, where we first met, got me through the proposal presentation and then fairly swiftly signed. Alice, you immediately got me, got what I was doing and I couldn't be more grateful for that.

To everyone at RPS, thank you, thank you, thank you! Cindy, you have given me so much confidence with your kindness and trust in my ability. Julia, your enthusiasm for my concept was so encouraging and I've loved having you as a support, particularly at the beginning of my journey. Leslie and Megs, I adored your vision for my book from the moment we began talking and it was so comforting to be on the same page from the get-go. Megs, you know how much I love the design of the book and it was a dream to have you on the shoot throughout. Miriam, last but definitely not least, thank you for your constant support, advice and help, and of course brilliant edit – I couldn't have asked for a lovelier editor. Thank you to Lizzie for managing the publicity, especially your advice and knowledge pre-sale.

To Clare Winfield for the stunning photography and everything that you brought to set. I love styling for your camera; your compositions and lighting are the dream and I couldn't be happier with what we've created together. Polly Webb-Wilson for the most perfect props, heavenly textures and ultimate colour combos. The best.

To Ells and Jojo for being such brilliant styling assistants, friends and kitchen mates for me throughout the shoot. Thank you so much.

There are so many women I could name that I look up to and have worked with in recent years, but I want to note a few that helped me right at the beginning. I started out un-trained, without much knowledge at

all and in great need of experience. Eleanor Maidment, Becks Woollard and Rosie Ramsden, you all got me on shoots, gave me recipe testing work and advice that I am eternally grateful for. The sisterhood of our industry continues to thrive because of women like you.

I wrote this book whilst trying to sell a house (during Brexit), buy a house, plan a wedding and somehow not go mad in the process, which I think (she says…) I've somehow managed. This is without a doubt down to the following: To my family, but especially my parents Angie and Peter, for your constant and unfailing support. To my closest and dearest (tasters and testers along the way) – Fi, Bryony, Lucy, Kate, Izzy, Anna, Nicky, Katy, Jules and Lotty… and some equally wonderful family testers: Summer, Harriet, Katie, Hugh, Wendy, Mimes and Vicki. I should also note Hewie, for turning up at least three nights a week during one testing stint to help hoover up surplus suppers, a tough but gallant role.

To Hal – you are my best friend, my (by the time this has been published) husband and the absolute, most experienced, most dedicated and most extraordinarily hungry taster. We are for many reasons, but that being one, made for each other. Forever may this perfect partnership thrive.